NIETZSCHE FOR ARCHITECTS

Nietzsche's philosophy is provocative and complex and has been hugely influential on modern intellectual history and European culture. But his critical approach and writing style invites misunderstandings, sometimes with disastrous consequences. His ideas—or those loosely associated with him—are often briefly cited in scholarly studies in architectural theory and history. His ideas are thought to have influenced the theories and designs of such iconic architects as Le Corbusier, Henry van de Velde, Bruno Taut, Louis H. Sullivan, Lebbeus Woods, and Peter Eisenman, as well as competing approaches to architecture and design, such as those adopted by the Bauhaus school and the Nazis. In the bewildering array of architectural positions that lay claim to Nietzsche as an influence, how can we begin to make sense of Nietzsche's own approach to architecture? And how can we identify within his complex philosophy the key ideas and themes we require to make sense of his contribution to architecture? This first introduction to Nietzsche's philosophy written specifically for architects locates his evaluation of appropriate and inappropriate architecture in the body of his writings and presents a clear overview of Nietzsche's insights into architectural design alongside his advice for architects and designers.

Lucy Huskinson is Professor of Philosophy at Bangor University, UK. Her interests lie in the intersections of philosophy, psychology, and architecture, and in the idea that buildings shape us as much as we shape them. She is author of several books in these fields, including *Architecture and the Mimetic Self: A Psychoanalytic Study of How Buildings Make and Break Our Lives* (2018) and *Nietzsche and Architecture: The Grand Style for Modern Living* (2024). Her books have been translated into Turkish, Serbian, and Portuguese.

'In this spirited, uplifting and assured book, Lucy Huskinson carefully and lucidly exposes Nietzsche's timely call to reanimate built form. As an invitation to "listeners and seekers" to transcend functionalism and spent symbolism, it lifts architecture from its contemporary malaise, reviving it as a vital agent of cultural ambition and personal introspection. This book is a fascinating read and essential for all those who are designing and building for the future.'

Dr. Martin Gledhill, *architect, senior lecturer in architecture, University of Bath, UK, and author of* The Bollingen Tower: Constructing a Jungian Sense of Place *(Routledge, 2026)*

'Architects will understand with Lucy Huskinson's eloquent study that art is not a result of a flourishing culture, but its fundamental requirement. Only a completely unchained "Will to Build" and a highly intense "dance of design" can focus our imagination on "an organic singleness of idea", required by the architectural framework of life lived as a total art. By recognizing "thinking as creating", our contemporary nihilistic culture, which is still fixated on "Being and Truth" can open itself to the vast potentials of eternal human "becoming" based on architecture understood as vigorous "science of fiction".'

Stephen Griek, *author of* Nietzsches Architektur der Erkennenden. Die Welt als Wissenschaft und Fiktion *(transcript: Bielefeld, 2023) and lecturer of philosophy of architecture at Geneva's University of Applied Sciences and Arts (HEPIA), Switzerland*

Thinkers for Architects

Series Editor: Adam Sharr, Newcastle University, UK

Editorial Board
Jonathan A. Hale, University of Nottingham, UK
Hilde Heynen, KU Leuven, Netherlands
David Leatherbarrow, University of Pennsylvania, USA

Architects have often looked to philosophers and theorists from beyond the discipline for design inspiration or in search of a critical framework for practice. This original series offers quick, clear introductions to key thinkers who have written about architecture and whose work can yield insights for designers.

"*Each unintimidatingly slim book makes sense of the subjects' complex theories.*"

Building Design

"*... a valuable addition to any studio space or computer lab.*"

Architectural Record

"*... a creditable attempt to present their subjects in a useful way.*"

Architectural Review

Kant for Architects
Diane Morgan

Freud for Architects
John Abell

Peirce for Architects
Richard Coyne

Latour for Architects
Albena Yaneva

Baudrillard for Architects
Francesco Proto

Stiegler for Architects
David Capener

For more information about this series, please visit: https://www.routledge.com/Thinkers-for-Architects/book-series/THINKARCH

Nietzsche
for
Architects

Lucy Huskinson

LONDON AND NEW YORK

First published 2026
by Routledge
4 Park Square, Milton Park, Abingdon, Oxon OX14 4RN

and by Routledge
605 Third Avenue, New York, NY 10158

Routledge is an imprint of the Taylor & Francis Group, an informa business

© 2026 Lucy Huskinson

The right of Lucy Huskinson to be identified as author of this work has been asserted in accordance with sections 77 and 78 of the Copyright, Designs and Patents Act 1988.

All rights reserved. No part of this book may be reprinted or reproduced or utilised in any form or by any electronic, mechanical, or other means, now known or hereafter invented, including photocopying and recording, or in any information storage or retrieval system, without permission in writing from the publishers.

Trademark notice: Product or corporate names may be trademarks or registered trademarks, and are used only for identification and explanation without intent to infringe.

British Library Cataloguing-in-Publication Data
A catalogue record for this book is available from the British Library

Library of Congress Cataloging-in-Publication Data
Names: Huskinson, Lucy, 1976- author.
Title: Nietzsche for architects / Lucy Huskinson.
Description: Abingdon, Oxon; New York, NY : Routledge, 2025. | Series: Thinkers for architects | Includes bibliographical references and index.
Identifiers: LCCN 2025000833 (print) | LCCN 2025000834 (ebook) |
ISBN 9781032591773 (hardback) | ISBN 9781032589084 (paperback) |
ISBN 9781003453345 (ebook)
Subjects: LCSH: Nietzsche, Friedrich Wilhelm, 1844–1900. | Architecture—Philosophy.
Classification: LCC B3317.H875 2025 (print) | LCC B3317 (ebook) |
DDC 193—dc23/eng/20250409
LC record available at https://lccn.loc.gov/2025000833
LC ebook record available at https://lccn.loc.gov/2025000834

ISBN: 9781032591773 (hbk)
ISBN: 9781032589084 (pbk)
ISBN: 9781003453345 (ebk)

DOI: 10.4324/9781003453345

Typeset in Frutiger
by codeMantra

Every effort has been made to contact copyright-holders. Please advise the publisher of any errors or omissions, and these will be corrected in subsequent editions.

For my mother, Janet

Contents

Series editor's preface   xi
Acknowledgements   xiii
Abbreviations of Nietzsche's works   xiv
List of illustrations   xv

1. Introduction   1

2. Placing Nietzsche's life and ideas through buildings and places   9

3. Decadent modern architecture. '*Amassed* rather than *assembled*'   24

   Last men and cultivated philistines: problems of excessive knowledge and its weak application   24
   Historicism and style-revivalism: the problem of relying on others for inspiration   27
   The need for a unifying instinct   29
   Architectural analogies of a declining culture   30
   Disembodied architecture, tricks, and superficial effects: Wagner's Festspielhaus in Bayreuth   33
   Architecture for the cultivated philistine   36

4. The will to power as a will to build   40

   Will to power   41
   Architects and will to power   43
   Designing with will to power: Henry van de Velde and Louis H. Sullivan   48
   The dance of design   52

Ornament: non-distracting, surface rhythms 55
Festive surfaces: Gottfried Semper 58
Beyond boundaries: designing for new heights and expanding horizons 62
German architecture for the German spirit? 69

5. Nietzsche's architects   71

Secular temple buildings 72
Semper's opera house: the first Nietzsche monument? 75
Nietzsche temples 78
Fritz Schumacher's temple (1898) 79
Henry van de Velde's temples (1909–13) 82
Building with glass and crystal: Bruno Taut and Peter Behrens 92
Nietzsche and Nazism 97
Nazi architecture 99
Reconciling Nietzsche and Nazism through architecture? The case of the Nietzsche Hall 102
The Nietzsche Hall, Weimar (1934–44) 106

Conclusion: Nietzschean lessons for architects   111

Recommended reading   117
References   119
Index   125

Series editor's preface

Adam Sharr

Architects have frequently looked to thinkers in philosophy and theory for design ideas, or in search of a critical framework for practice. Yet architects and students of architecture can struggle to navigate thinkers' writings. It can be daunting to approach original texts with little appreciation of their contexts. And existing introductions seldom explore a thinker's architectural material in detail. So this original series offers clear, quick and accurate introductions to key thinkers who have written about architecture. Each book summarises what a thinker has to offer for architects. It locates their architectural thinking in their wider body of work, introduces significant books and essays, helps decode terms, and provides a quick reference for further reading. If you find philosophical and theoretical writing about architecture difficult, or just don't know where to begin, this series is indispensable.

Books in the *Thinkers for Architects* series come out of architecture. They pursue architectural modes of understanding, aiming to introduce a thinker to an architectural audience. Each thinker has a unique and distinctive ethos, and the structure of each book derives from the character at its focus. The thinkers explored are prodigious writers so any short introduction can only address a fraction of their work. Each author—an architect or architectural critic—has focused on a selection of a thinker's writings that they judge most relevant to designers and interpreters of architecture. These books will therefore be the first point of reference, rather than the last word, about a particular thinker for architects. It is hoped that the books will encourage you to read further, inviting you to delve deeper into the writings of a particular thinker.

The *Thinkers for Architects* series is now in its second decade. Books published so far have mostly covered so-called canonical figures: well-established names from the traditions—the 'canons'—of philosophy and critical and cultural theory, who have long influenced architecture and architects. Like in most academic and professional fields, such names have historically been largely Western, white, and male. This reflects the structures of power and influence that typically determine who can access education, publishing, reviews, and the kinds of jobs that give people space to think and write. We live at a time when populist politics are on the rise in various countries around the globe. Some governments, and certain media organisations, are weaponising intolerance of differences between people for political ends. Against this context, it grows ever more urgent to appreciate who is—and who is not—typically able to speak to a public audience, and to diversify the reference points of academic disciplines and professions like architecture. From the start, *Thinkers for Architects* has always been concerned with ideas that challenge traditional canons. Having covered many long-established thinkers, the series now seeks to engage a wider range of voices. Alongside familiar names, it will increasingly introduce thinkers who are less familiar to architects, but whose ideas have equal potential for designers. For example, as well as books covering Georgio Agamben, Hannah Arendt, Graham Harman, and Bernard Stiegler, planned volumes will examine the architectural thinking of Franz Fanon, Stuart Hall, Donna Harraway, McKenzie Wark, and Simone Weil. The series continues to expand, aiming to explore exciting and diverse thinkers who have something to say to architects.

Adam Sharr is Professor of Architecture at Newcastle University, UK, and editor-in-chief of *arq: Architectural Research Quarterly* published by Cambridge University Press. He practises with Design Office, which was included in the *Architects Journal* '40 under 40' listing of 'the UK's most exciting emerging architectural talent' in 2020. Adam is author or editor of eight books on architecture, including *Heidegger for Architects* and *Reading Architecture and Culture* published by Routledge.

Acknowledgements

Over the years, I have had many opportunities to present and share my ideas on Nietzsche and architecture at conferences and guest lectures, and I'm grateful for the lively discussions they have sparked. But I most thankful for the conversations with my inquisitive students, which are always fun and thought provoking.

I deeply appreciate the support and friendly banter I have with my colleagues—especially with the following free spirits: Peter Shapely, Josh Andrews, Gareth Evans-Jones, Farhaan Wali, Steve Nash, Hayley Roberts, Tracy Williams, Bethan Loftus, and Lisa Sparkes; Roderick Main and Mark Saban.

Special thanks must go to Fran Ford, Hannah Studd and Adam Guppy at Routledge for accompanying me throughout the publication process; to Susan Leaper at Florence Production for her thoughtful and attentive copyediting; Stephen Griek for his comments; and to Adam Sharr, the editor of 'Thinkers for Architects' for establishing this brilliant book series.

Above all, my deepest gratitude goes to Jeff, Mark, and Ludo, and the adventures we have.

Lucy Huskinson
Darkest North Wales
Winter 2025

Abbreviations of Nietzsche's works

AC   *The Antichrist* (1895). Cited with aphorism number.
AML   *Aus meinem Leben* (1854–69). Cited with page number.
BGE   *Beyond Good and Evil* (1886). Cited with aphorism number.
BT   *The Birth of Tragedy* (1872). Cited with section number.
BVN   Sämtliche Briefe (Kritische Studienausgabe). Cited with letter number and page number.
CW   *The Case of Wagner* (1888). Cited with section number.
D   *Dawn* (1881). Cited with aphorism number.
EH   *Ecce Homo* (written in 1888, published in 1908). Cited with chapter number, book title abbreviation, and section number.
FS   *Frühe Schriften: Jugendschriften* (1854–69). Cited with volume and page reference.
GM   *On the Genealogy of Morality* (1887). Cited with treatise number and section number.
GMD   *The Greek Music Drama* (1870). Cited with page number.
GS   *The Gay Science* (1882). Cited with aphorism number.
GSA   Goethe Schiller Archiv, Weimar.
HHI   *Human, All Too Human I* (1878). Cited with aphorism number.
KSA   Sämtliche Werke (*Kritische Studienausgabe*). Cited with volume, fragment number, and page reference.
KSB   Sämtliche Briefe (*Kritische Studienausgabe*). Cited with volume, letter number, and page reference.
TI   *Twilight of the Idols* (1888). Cited with chapter number, section number, and page reference.
UM   *Untimely Meditations* (1873–76). Cited with essay number and section number.
WS   *The Wanderer and His Shadow* (1880). Cited with aphorism number.
Z   *Thus Spoke Zarathustra* (1883–85). Cited with part number, chapter number, section number, and page reference.

Illustrations

1 Galleria Subalpina, Turin (built 1873–74, Pietro Carrera). Interior. Looking towards Nietzsche's apartment. Author's photograph. 19
2 Palazzo Pitti, Florence (built 1458, Luca Fancelli). Front elevation. Postcard c.1910. 53
3 Mole Antonelliana, Turin (built 1863–89, Alessandro Antonelli). Front elevation. Author's photograph. 66
4 Nietzsche-Denkmal. Tempel des Lebens/Temple of Life (1898, Fritz Schumacher). Charcoal sketch. 80
5 Ernst Abbe-Denkmal, Jena (built 1908–11, Henry van de Velde). Exterior view from the south. Author's photograph. 85
6 Villa Silberblick, Nietzsche-Archiv building, Weimar (renovations 1902–3, Henry van de Velde). Front elevation. Author's photograph. 86
7 Nietzsche temple design for Weimar (1912, Henry van de Velde). Third design. Perspective sketch. Collection ENSAV—La Cambre, Bruxelles, inv.1508. © Henry van de Velde. 86
8 Villa Silberblick, Weimar. Nietzsche-archiv main room with Nietzsche herm (1905, Max Klinger). Detailing vertical wooden strips and cavetto moulding by Henry van de Velde. Author's photograph. 87
9 Nietzsche temple design for Weimar (1912, Henry van de Velde). Final design. Perspective sketch. Collection ENSAV—La Cambre, Bruxelles, inv.1508. © Henry van de Velde. 91
10 *Hamburger Vorhalle*, Exposition of the Decorative Arts, Turin (built 1902, Peter Behrens). © Bildarchiv Foto Marburg. 94
11 *Monument des Neuen Gesetzes* (1919, Bruno Taut). Illustrated letter with a drawing of a project for the Monument to the Dead. © Canadian Center for Architecture. 96

12 Nietzsche Memorial Hall, Weimar (built 1934–44, Paul Schultze-Naumburg). Model, with figures of Apollo and Dionysus flanking the main entrance. Photograph, January 1937. © Goethe und Schiller Archiv. Photo: Klassik Stiftung Weimar. GSA 72/2610.   107

CHAPTER 1

Introduction

Nietzsche stands as a towering figure of our times. His ideas have profoundly shaped modern Western thought as a cultural critic and forerunner of postmodernism, with its rejection of universal truths and endorsement of multiple and competing perspectives. Given his far-reaching impact, it is not surprising that his philosophy is believed to have shaped the work of leading architects in the modern era such as Le Corbusier, Ludwig Mies van der Rohe, Peter Behrens, Bruno Taut, Henry van de Velde, Louis H. Sullivan, Lebbeus Woods, and Peter Eisenman, among others. Although no prominent female architects are widely known to have explicitly cited Nietzsche as an influence, several worked within intellectual environments where his ideas were influential. The work of such figures such as Zaha Hadid, Lina Bo Bardi, Denise Scott Brown, and Elizabeth Diller can be interpreted through a Nietzschean lens.

At the same time, Nietzsche's legacy is controversial. Some dismiss him as a madman with eccentric, incredulous, or even dangerous ideas. Those who hold such views probably have not given his thought the serious attention it demands and may only have a passing familiarity with it. And here lies a problem. Nietzsche's philosophy is notoriously difficult to interpret, has frequently been misunderstood, and is sometimes wildly misrepresented and misappropriated. Nietzsche himself was aware of this challenge, as evidenced by the final sentence of his last book, *Ecce Homo*, where he tentatively asks, 'Have I been understood?'.

Why is Nietzsche's philosophy so often misunderstood? A major reason is his cryptic writing style, which is filled with metaphors, analogies, and ambiguities, sometimes deliberately obscure, dense, and misleading. This is particularly evident in his aphorisms—short passages ranging from a single sentence to several pages—which, when read together or consecutively, can express contradictory ideas, leaving readers confused rather than enlightened. Nietzsche used this style to encourage his readers to consider a variety of different perspectives and to reflect on which are most compelling. His aim was to help us identify the values that drive us, both personally and culturally, and to examine our reasons for holding them. At times, Nietzsche seemed to want to shock his readers, challenging their deeply held beliefs and values in hopes of revealing how these ideas are rooted in unhelpful ideological systems of thought that have taken hold of our cultural outlook and dictate how we live.

Nietzsche deliberately avoided systematic thinking and committing himself to singular perspectives, which can be especially frustrating when trying to pinpoint his views on specific subjects. This holds true in the case of architecture and the built environment, where Nietzsche doesn't offer a clear, comprehensive philosophy or a set of design principles for architects to follow. In fact, some might argue that he says very little about architecture at all. While there is a substantial body of work exploring Nietzsche's relationship with aesthetics and art, only very few scholars have examined the connections between his philosophical ideas and architectural theory or applied his ideas to architectural designs. (In the recommended reading section of this book, I highlight some useful studies and sources.) Nietzsche's explicit references to architecture are scant and scattered across his writings. However, when considered alongside his broader discussions—such as his exploration of the power of aesthetics to transform the onlooker, his thoughts on historicism and style, and his emphasis on creativity through his concept of the will to power (which I will explain later)—we discover that he had quite a lot to say about architectural design after all. Additionally, his personal letters to colleagues, friends, and family, where he shared his impressions of various cities and buildings, offer a rich source of insight into his thinking on architecture, suggesting the beginnings of a distinct theory about the cultural and existential importance of the built environment, as well as the merits and pitfalls of specific building types and design elements.

Nietzsche's work is a complex and eloquent mix of self-contradiction—a fact Nietzsche himself acknowledged when he wrote, 'This thinker needs no one to refute him: he does that for himself' (WS.249). The many contrasting perspectives within Nietzsche's work result in numerous interpretations of his philosophy. As historian Steven E. Aschheim points out, one can extract intellectual support from Nietzsche's writings for almost any ideological position, including anarchist, expressionist, feminist, misogynist, futurist, nationalist, Nazi, sexual-libertarian, socialist, völkisch, Zionist, Catholic, Protestant, deconstructionist, postmodernist, vegetarian, and more.

Given Nietzsche's ambiguous and elusive writing style, and the 'pick-and-mix' approach it often encourages in readers, it is perhaps unsurprising that his ideas have been interpreted in various ways by modern architects and their commentators, and sometimes skewed to fit their own aspirations and agendas. For instance, Nietzsche's championing of 'empty forms', when taken to mean forms devoid of ornamentation or historical reference, has been used to justify philosophically the aesthetic values of the Bauhaus school of design, architecture and applied arts (1919–33) and radical, modernist 'international' styles (1920s–1970s). These styles often emphasise simplicity, featuring large expanses of glass and blank white surfaces to highlight their construction materials and functional aspects of the building.

On the other hand, Nietzsche has also been invoked as an inspiration for the use of decorative ornamentation. In homage to Nietzsche, architects like Peter Behrens incorporated symbolic motifs from Nietzsche's most popular work, *Thus Spoke Zarathustra*, into their designs, such as in his 'Zarathustra house' (1901) in Darmstadt, Germany, and his Hamburger Vorhalle (1902), designed for the German section of the International Exhibition of Modern Decorative Art in Turin. Similarly, Bruno Taut's sketch for a glass monument (1919) was meant to represent 'new laws', and new ways of being following the Great War, incorporating a quotation from this book.

Determining which of these opposing design approaches—minimalist or ornamental—is more representative of Nietzsche's ideas is difficult. Would Nietzsche have supported ornamentation or rejected it? Situating him within specific architectural traditions is tricky, if not futile. Further complicating matters, Nietzsche's call to revive the German spirit in modern culture has been interpreted by some as a rejection of modernist styles in favour of historical forms rooted in German folk traditions. His name has subsequently been invoked to justify philosophically the eradication of so-called 'degenerate' and 'Bolshevik' architecture and to endorse designs suited to the Third Reich of Nazi Germany, which favoured a mishmash of contradictory styles, including Albert Speer's infamous grandiose plans for Germania, the envisioned capital city of the world.

Numerous architectural historians have briefly referenced Nietzsche's ideas in their work, usually for readers interested in architectural history and theory. However, these references are often simplified and inaccurate, particularly when discussing his most popular and frequently misunderstood concepts—the Übermensch (or superman) and the will to power. I will explore these ideas throughout this book, but it is helpful to note now that the Übermensch represents Nietzsche's notion of a highly creative individual who lives authentically according to self-made values, and the will to power is the driving force that helps that person to overcome challenges and obstacles to their creativity. It is understandable that these texts tend to focus less on Nietzsche's philosophy itself, often mentioning his ideas only because certain architects have cited him as an influence or because their work aligns loosely with his broader philosophical vision of elevating culture through creative design.

Earlier I mentioned that Nietzsche is sometimes dismissed as a 'mad' scholar. Indeed, he is thought to have succumbed to 'madness' after a lifetime of debilitating symptoms, including chronic migraines, insomnia, vomiting, digestive issues, poor eyesight, delusions, manic episodes, and eventual paralysis. Themes of suffering, sickness, and health feature prominently in his writings. While Nietzsche himself occasionally cuts a rather pathetic figure, plagued by continual illness, depression, and loneliness, his philosophy envisions the rise of noble individuals who embody great health and optimum creativity.

<u>Nietzsche is often associated with terminology and catchphrases that, when taken out of context, contribute to a distorted and unsavoury caricature of him as someone with grandiose cravings for power.</u>

Phrases like 'will to power', 'God is dead', 'the superman', 'philosophising with a hammer', 'nihilism', The Antichrist (Nietzsche, 1895/2021), and 'master morality' might, on their own, suggest the promotion of destructive, ego-driven ideals of domination through brute force. However, this interpretation is far from accurate when viewed in the proper context of Nietzsche's critique of modernity with his desire to eliminate so-called defective and corrupting values.

As I will explore throughout this book, Nietzsche's concept of the superman is about exercising the will to power as an act of inner strength, applied to oneself rather than others. Similarly, when he proclaimed the death of God—referring to the elimination of absolute, universal truths in favour of individuals crafting their own values and meanings—his intention was not to plunge society into anarchy or passive nihilism. Instead, he saw it as a liberating moment, a new, level playing field that offered some people the exciting opportunity to lead richer, more meaningful lives and to create with greater authenticity. Nietzsche's philosophy does not culminate in nihilism with the death of God—it begins there. In other words, when Nietzsche philosophically 'destroys with a hammer', he aims to raze to the ground all outmoded values that hinder the flourishing of individuals and cultures in the present. His philosophy is deeply concerned with how we can thrive, create, and design in ways that empower ourselves and society.

Although Nietzsche would argue that there is no single, correct way to design, nor a specific architectural style or blueprint for excellence, he is often unfairly linked to grandiose, monumental, and oppressive designs. While there is no distinct 'Nietzschean' architectural style, his ideas and personal reflections suggest he favoured designs that contrast starkly to this exaggerated and misleading image. Nietzsche appreciated architecture that conveyed power, not through overwhelming physical features, but by encouraging us to reflect on our own presence in relation to the structure. For Nietzsche, effective architectural design invites us to engage with the interplay play of forms, textures, and spaces, and in such a way that we become more attuned to ourselves, and more aware of our connection to the built environment, thereby grounding us more fully in the physical world.

This book does not claim to present yet another 'correct' interpretation of Nietzsche's philosophy, nor does it attempt to argue that Nietzsche was a closet architect or architectural theorist. The core of Nietzsche's thought lies in the creative tensions between multiple interpretations, and the key to understanding him is through a person's own subjective responses to his writings. However, this does not mean that Nietzsche's ideas are immune to misinterpretation or that any one interpretation is as valid as another. In fact, Nietzsche sought to overcome the lazy, nihilistic attitude of 'anything goes'.

Perhaps the most notorious misunderstanding and misappropriation of Nietzsche's work—which has left a lasting stain on his reputation, especially for those only superficially familiar with his philosophy—came from the German National Socialist Party.

The Nazis distorted Nietzsche's concept of the Übermensch, twisting the idea of self-mastery into their notion of a biological 'master race' of the Third Reich. This perversion of Nietzsche's ideas overlooks the fact that he vigorously opposed unrestrained German nationalism, mocked the notion of a Teutonic master race, and despised anti-Semitism in all its forms. Unfortunately, this twisted version of Nietzschean philosophy was popularised by his entrepreneurial fascist younger sister, Elisabeth Förster-Nietzsche.

Elisabeth had close ties with the Nazi Party, having befriended Hitler, who attended her funeral in 1935, and married the anti-Semitic activist, Bernhard Förster, with whom she attempted to create a 'pure' Aryan republic in Paraguay, called 'Nueva Germania' or 'New Germany'. After Nietzsche's death, Elisabeth took control of his extensive archive of unpublished writings and notes, appointing herself as the sole executor of his literary estate. With financial support and publicity from the Nazi Party, she worked to cultivate a 'cult following' around a mythologised image of her brother as a prophetic hero of a new Germany.

This book seeks to clarify Nietzsche's constructive ideas about architecture, and to rescue his philosophy from persistent misunderstandings. At the same time, it recognises that Nietzsche's architectural legacy also encompasses the many ways his ideas have been misinterpreted and misused, including when they have been twisted into opposing or even monstrous forms. Just as Nietzsche's ideas resist systematisation, the chapters in this book do not have to be read in linear order. They explore themes that illuminate his contribution to architecture. You can dip into the chapters as you would with Nietzsche's aphorisms or read the book cover to cover as you might with Nietzsche's most popular work, *Thus Spoke Zarathustra* (1883–5).

Chapter 2, 'Placing Nietzsche's life and ideas through buildings and places', explores Nietzsche's nomadic lifestyle and his deep connections with various cities and landscapes. It examines how his observations on the environments he visited and inhabited shaped his philosophy. While Nietzsche is popularly portrayed as a solitary wanderer in the mountains, he was also deeply engaged with urban spaces, and his thoughts on architecture influenced many of his key ideas, providing him with metaphors central to this thinking. On the one hand, I consider how his negative impressions of modern German architecture contributed to his broader critique of the decline of modern culture. On the other, I examine how his admiration for buildings like the grand palazzi in Genoa, the Palazzo Pitti in Florence, and the Mole Antonelliana in Turin informed his vision of cultural renewal through more creative architectural designs rooted in the exercise of will to power. The principles underlying Nietzsche's attraction to these structures offer a framework for understanding what a 'Nietzschean architecture' might entail.

Chapter 3, 'Decadent modern architecture: "*Amassed* rather than *assembled*"', delves deeper into Nietzsche's critique of modern German architecture. He argued that at the heart of Germany's decaying culture lay a deep-seated 'will to truth', a desire to explain and improve life at the expense of more spontaneous and instinctual ways of being. This, Nietzsche claimed, desensitises people to their surroundings and leads to the creation of uninspiring art and architecture that incorporates a mishmash of styles with little conviction or cohesive artistic expression. The revivalist styles popular in nineteenth-century Germany, according to Nietzsche, symbolise a failure to innovate, producing buildings that imitate the past without addressing contemporary needs. He used architectural metaphors to illustrate how modern German culture is stifled in its over-reliance on rationality and its suppression of instinctual creativity. He introduced the concept of the 'cultivated philistine', a figure who shuns imaginative risks in favour of clinging to outdated traditions. This character serves as a symbol of the cultural stagnation Nietzsche deplored. Richard Wagner, whom Nietzsche described as the 'modern artist par excellence' is presented as another emblem of this decline—an artist who, in Nietzsche's view, valued theatrical spectacle over artistic substance. Nietzsche associated the cultivated philistine with a garden pavilion that is structurally flawed but extravagantly furnished, and he links Wagner to the labyrinth, a metaphor for the complex and confused state of modern souls. I further examine how Wagner's Festspielhaus (Festival Theatre) in Bayreuth, a theatre designed for his musical performances, epitomises the troubled split between intellect and instinct in modern culture.

Nietzsche suggested that buildings should foster self-reflection rather than distract with the 'chatter' of historical styles.

He believed architects should strive to unify the Apollonian approach to art—which was the prevailing approach in modern Germany, with its emphasis on restraint, order, and structure—with a Dionysian approach to incorporate more instinctual, fluid, and expressive elements into their designs. Chapter 4, 'The will to power as a will to build', explores these aspects of Nietzsche's constructive philosophy, which are grounded in his notion of the will to power. When architecture aligns with the will to power, it will radiate vitality and exhibit a unified style, free from the constraints of historical imitation. I examine how this idea of will to power resonates with the work of architects associated with Nietzsche, such as Henry van de Velde, with his concept of 'line force' as a rhythmic, uplifting dance of forms, Louis H. Sullivan's use of ornament to invigorate and animate structures, Gottfried Semper's festive surfaces, and Alessandro Antonelli's relentless pursuit to innovate and build ever higher.

Although Nietzsche himself criticised the idea of monuments built in his honour, several architectural projects were planned and commissioned to celebrate his ideas. In Chapter 5, 'Nietzsche's architects', I assess whether these designs align with Nietzsche's own principles for good architecture. Finally, in the conclusion, I offer some Nietzschean advice for aspiring architects.

CHAPTER 2

Placing Nietzsche's life and ideas through buildings and places

The places we inhabit can offer insight into our interior landscapes, our desires, beliefs, ideas, and feelings. For many, this connection is found in their home, particularly in rooms or spaces where they feel intimately connected, grounded, and 'in place'. As the French philosopher Gaston Bachelard observed in *The Poetics of Space* (1957), 'On whatever theoretical horizon we examine it, the house image would appear to have become the topography of our intimate being' (1957/1994: xxxvi). For others, a deep connection with place happens outside, perhaps within the countryside or within the bustling energy of a familiar town or city. Nietzsche found such a connection through his nomadic lifestyle, moving between diverse environments, specifically between Alpine mountains and the urban landscapes of various European cities. And one building, in particular, held special meaning for him and was one to which he felt most intimately connected—the Mole Antonelliana, a structure that towered over the streets of Turin. I will return to this significant building later but, for now, it is important to note how Nietzsche's nomadic lifestyle reflected not only his desire to alleviate his physical ailments by taking advantage of different climates, but also a fundamental feature of his philosophy—his belief that creativity and life itself emerge from the tension of competing perspectives.

Friedrich Wilhem Nietzsche was born on 15 October 1844 in the small farming village of Röcken, near Leipzig in Saxony, in the parsonage where his father served as the village parson. His first house left a lasting impression on him, one that arguably stayed with him throughout his life. In an autobiographical account written at the age of 15, Nietzsche described the profound impression of this house, echoing ideas later expressed by Bachelard a hundred years later about how 'the house we were born in' becomes 'inscribed in us', so that even 'the feel of the tiniest latch [remains] in our hands' (1957/1994: 6, 14–15). Nietzsche wrote:

> [I]f any image were to escape my soul, the one I could not possibly forget would be the familiar parsonage building. For it has been engraved in my soul with a mighty stylus. The house was built only in 1820 and was therefore in very nice condition. Several steps led up to the first floor. I can still remember the study on the top floor. Rows of books, many illustrated works among them, these tomes made this spot one of my favourite places. A garden of grass and fruit trees stretched out behind the house. A part of it would be under water in the spring, so usually the cellar was flooded too. The courtyard extended in front of the house with the barn and stable building and led to the flower garden. I often rested on the arbour or on the benches.
>
> (AML.3)

Beside the house of his early childhood stood his father's church—a twelfth-century Romanesque building with a fortified tower—where Nietzsche would later be buried alongside his mother and sister. Born into a long line of Lutheran ministers, Nietzsche was expected to continue this tradition.

As a young child he earned the nickname 'little pastor' for his ability to recite scripture and religious songs with great emotion. When he was nearly five, his father died after a fall, and his mother soon relocated the family to Naumburg. In an early autobiographical account, Nietzsche spoke of his 'love of architecture', describing how, at a young age, he constructed model buildings. Through 'much practice', he learnt 'all the finer points of building', constructing small chapels, and later more elaborate creations, such as 'magnificent temples' with 'rows of columns, high towers with winding staircases, mines with underground lakes and interior lighting, and finally castles' (FS.1: 152).

He also recounted how captivated he was by the family's move from rural Röcken to the more urban Naumburg, with its 'beautiful wide streets with ancient houses', and especially its marketplace, which featured a fountain and large town hall. 'How big it is! What grandeur!' he wrote. 'Let me always look at it with awe.' While he praised the 'high, venerable city church' that 'protrudes' to the left of the town hall, he was scathing of the parsonage in front of it, exclaiming, 'See the miserable building standing there! Oh, if it were torn away, does it not inhibit the whole view of the church?!' (FS.1:7: 16–18).

At the age of 14, Nietzsche was awarded a scholarship to Schulpforta, an esteemed preparatory school located in a Cistercian monastery, where he was expected to train for the clergy. There, he excelled in religious studies, German literature, and classical studies. He went on to read theology and classical philology at the University of Bonn (which at the time focused on the interpretation of biblical and classical texts). However, after one semester, Nietzsche lost his Christian faith and abandoned theology, much to his mother's distress. He then transferred to Leipzig University to focus on philology. As a student, Nietzsche felt a distance from his fellow students, believing that his own sense of purpose in life was at odds with the pursuits and interests of those around him. Over time, he came to view solitude as essential for creativity.

Nietzsche devoted much of his work to criticising Christianity, which he regarded as a toxic ideological system that enslaved people with its corrupt values and fabricated truths. He believed that Christianity, along with all ideological systems, pursued a 'will to truth'—the misguided belief that life could be explained, improved, and corrected. Nietzsche argued that this flawed approach had deeply infiltrated modern European culture, becoming so ingrained in society that it would take centuries to free ourselves from its stranglehold. He advocated for a more life-affirming and productive approach to life. The will to truth prioritises reason and progress over human instinct and more spontaneous, creative values. This, Nietzsche claimed, leads to culture stagnation and decadence, alienating people from their creative instincts and desensitising them to the natural world. The overemphasis on reason in the search of a supposedly 'correct' way of living had established an unnatural divide between our internal lives—which have become cluttered with needless information and knowledge—and the tangible, sensory reality around us. In this state, we are unable to create in meaningful ways; instead, our designs and works become sterile, abstract, and lifeless, failing to engage or inspire those who encounter them.

Nietzsche addressed this issue by highlighting an unhealthy imbalance between two approaches to life: the Apollonian, which emphasises rationality, structure, and order, and the Dionysian, which embraces disorder, chaos, rapture, and the dissolution of boundaries. He argued that

the Dionysian alone is dangerous, as it shatters subjectivity, and must be contained by the Apollonian for creative expression. Similarly, the Apollonian requires the Dionysian for nourishment and renewal.

Nietzsche believed that the antidote to the modern mindset's unnatural split lies in adopting the aesthetic approach of the ancient Greeks, who mastered a creative balance of these impulses in their tragic plays. These tragedies, by confronting the audience with life's uncertainties and sufferings, encouraged a joyful affirmation of existence and reduced the need for comforting illusions or false ideologies. Nietzsche viewed ancient Greek tragedy as the highest expression of art and creative living, seeing the potential for a reunion of Apollonian and Dionysian perspectives to resensitise modern individuals to their material environments and imbue their creative designs with instinctual vitality and energy.

While studying at Leipzig University, Nietzsche met the German composer Richard Wagner, and this encounter marked the beginning of a relationship that would become tumultuous and painful for Nietzsche. At first, Nietzsche admired Wagner, regarding him as a genius capable of revitalising German culture through his operatic music, much like the ancient Greek tragedies, which combined history, myth, and a union of Apollonian and Dionysian forces. In his early work, *The Birth of Tragedy: Out of the Spirit of Music* (1872), Nietzsche proposed a culture grounded in art and the revival of tragedy, and he dedicated the book to Wagner. Nietzsche enthusiastically promoted Wagner's music and helped him to secure government funding for the construction of the Bayreuth theatre, envisioned as a grand venue for Wagner's works. The grand festival to open the theatre in 1876 was hotly anticipated by Nietzsche as an event to signal the beginning of Germany's artistic and cultural renewal. However, the festival proved disastrous for Nietzsche. Rather than inspiring cultural rebirth, it seemed to be a decadent, self-indulgent, and artificial display—precisely the problems it was meant to overcome. Disillusioned, Nietzsche fled the theatre, and his friendship with Wagner quickly deteriorated thereafter. It was at this time that Nietzsche began to lose trust in the transformative power of music. He came to view music as unreliable, prone to leading people astray with superficial emotions or fleeting flights of fancy, rather than bringing about the fundamental cultural renewal he envisioned. Instead, Nietzsche found comfort in the physical immediacy of architecture, which he saw as a more trustworthy remedy to the cultural problem. Architecture, in his view, could ground individuals in the material world while offering opportunities for Dionysian expression through the rhythmic interplay of its design features and forms.

Nietzsche was appointed professor of classical philology—the study of language in historical oral and written sources—at Basel University in 1869 at the remarkably young age of 24 years old, making him the youngest tenured academic in that post. However, his time there was brief. In 1876, the same year his relationship with Wagner ended, the university granted him a full year of sick leave. He remained in post for only four more years, retiring early due to ill health. Nietzsche used his retirement pension to fund his nomadic lifestyle, writing when his symptoms permitted. Despite his illness, this nomadic period proved highly productive, allowing him to write 11 works, including *Thus Spoke Zarathustra* (1883–5). His wandering existence seemed to fuel his creativity, yet Nietzsche was keenly aware of the isolation, insecurity, and uncertainty that often accompany a creative life—ideas he explored in his philosophy but struggled to accept fully in his personal life. In a letter to his friend Franz Overbeck in 1887, Nietzsche expressed his deep loneliness, writing, 'It hurts frightfully that in these fifteen years not one single person has "discovered" me, has needed me, has loved me.'

Thus Spoke Zarathustra has played a key role in popularising the romantic image of Nietzsche as a solitary wanderer, traversing treacherous paths of self-discovery.

This philosophical work of fiction, often poetic in style and filled with metaphor and ambiguity (as reflected in its subtitle, *A Book for Everyone and No One*), is considered a parody of the Bible. Its protagonist, Zarathustra parallels Jesus in many ways. Both figures leave their mountain caves at the age of 30 to spread their teachings to those who are willing to listen. However, while Jesus offers glad tidings, Zarathustra's 'good news' is that God is dead, and humans are now free to create their own identities. Unlike Jesus, Zarathustra does not seek to recruit disciples, as doing so would miss the point of his message.

The book became extremely popular in the early twentieth century, sparking intellectual discussions across European cafés and salons. A special 'field edition' was even distributed to German soldiers to carry in their backpacks during World War I. Architects of the time who read Nietzsche likely dipped into *Thus Spoke Zarathustra*, and its rousing call for artists to create a new style and world order may have inspired many architects to view Nietzsche as an influence. Zarathustra's words, 'O my brothers, I direct and consecrate you to a new nobility: you shall become begetters and cultivators and sowers of the future' (Z.III.12 [12]: 220) could have resonated with modern architects who saw themselves as heroic creators, capable of reviving culture through innovative design. Indeed, it has been suggested that architects like Le Corbusier and Louis H. Sullivan were influenced by *Thus Spoke Zarathustra* and may have sought to emulate its prophetic tone in their own writings, modelling themselves on the figure of Zarathustra—an idea revisited in Chapter 6 of this book.

It is important to recognise that both Nietzsche and his fictional spokesperson, Zarathustra, did not confine their travels or walks to the countryside or rural areas. Nietzsche belonged to a long tradition of philosophers who believed that walking was essential for clear and productive thinking. He famously stated, 'only ideas *won by walking* have value' (TI.I.34). While scholars have largely documented his walks in nature, less attention has been given to the significance of his regular walks through urban areas and the observations he made about the buildings he encountered along the way. Nietzsche was a keen observer of city life, frequently visiting cafés and theatres, and he was both a critic and admirer of architectural forms. In this respect, he was as much a *flâneur* of city streets as he was a wanderer in nature.

Nietzsche's comments on buildings and urban landscapes reveal both praise and criticism of architectural styles and features. He often critiqued buildings that were heavy with historical elements, powerful in the past but now seemingly out of place, distracting viewers and encouraging an intellectual, detached response. These buildings, which he saw as fostering the problematic split in the modern mindset, are distinctly Apollonian in form. In contrast, Nietzsche celebrated buildings that exuded a Dionysian energy, instinctively enlivening the onlooker and fostering self-reflection and a sense of connection to oneself. In Chapter 4, I will explain how, for Nietzsche, this type of architecture embodies the architect's will to power—a power that captures and organises the spirit of the times by merging Dionysian instincts within an Apollonian framework for others to experience and engage with.

Like Zarathustra, who lived in a cave high up in the mountains and held a dismissive view of town dwellers who live in low, stunted buildings (a theme I will revisit in the next chapter),

Nietzsche preferred architecture that drew the eye (and body) upwards. He often chose to live in high apartments with lofty ceilings and expansive views.

After fleeing the Wagner festival in Bayreuth, he found refuge in Sorrento, staying in a large room on the third floor of Villa Rubinacci. Although he described it to his sister as 'not an elegant villa', he noted that he had 'a very large room with a high ceiling and a terrace' offering views of the Isle of Ischia and Mount Vesuvius (KSB.5.565: 197). In 1880, while living in Venice, Nietzsche rented an apartment in Pallazo Berlendis, a seventeenth-century Neo-classical building at the end of Rio dei Mendicanti. In postcards to his mother, he described a 'grand staircase' leading up to the apartment, with its 'high room', and a ceiling that soared '22 feet high', which he believed improved his sleep. The apartment also offered a distant view of San Michele, 'Island of the Dead' (KSB.6.18: 13–14; KSB.6.20: 15). A year later, in Genoa, Nietzsche rented an attic room in Salita delle Battistine 8, situated near the bottom of a steep, cobbled street. He wrote to his mother and sister, expressing his delight in the 'very bright room, very high room—which is good for my mood', and its 'distant views of the sea and mountains' (KSB.6.181: 151).

Upward movement and expansive views towards the horizon express the will to power, reflecting a desire to transcend conventional boundaries, take risks, experiment, innovate, and create anew. Nietzsche was also drawn to the grandeur of Italian palazzi—impressive public buildings or private residences—which he saw as spatial manifestations of the will to power. He may have longed to live in a palazzo himself, as he fancifully described his lodgings in Genoa to his sister as being located on a 'steep street of palaces'. In reality, his house, like others on the street, was a rather modest terrace house of four to five storeys, quite different to the imposing palazzi lining Strada Nuova (now Via Garibaldi), just a short walk from his apartment.

Nietzsche admired these tall Baroque townhouses, which were built for wealthy Genoese merchants at the peak of their maritime power in the late sixteenth and early seventeenth centuries. In his book *The Gay Science* (1882) (or *Joyful Wisdom*), which he began writing in Genoa, he described these palazzi and the noble spirit of their creators. He saw each building as an embodiment of the 'virile force' of upright noblemen, masters of their craft, who celebrated life through the enduring strength of their buildings. As Nietzsche observed, these men built not simply for the present moment but to leave a lasting legacy: 'They have *lived* and wish to live on—that is what they are telling me with their houses, built and adorned to last for centuries and not for the fleeting hour.'

He imagined the builder gazing across everything he had constructed, from the city to the sea and mountains, 'and how with his gaze he exerts' a 'conquering power; he wants to fit all this into *his* plan and finally make it his *possession* by incorporating it into *his* plan'. Each palazzo, Nietzsche believed, reflected the singular vision and mastery of its creator: 'a singular taste that set itself apart from its neighbour as distinctive and self-sufficient'. He admired the healthy competition among these buildings, each displaying unique variations while together forming an overarching unity of style. For Nietzsche, they collectively embodied a 'loathing for the tedium of laws, and a will to overcome them', expressing a 'thirst for something new', and the ambition to 'set up a new world alongside the old' (GS.291).

Nietzsche loved Genoa, describing it to his mother and sister as a city that gave him 'peace and being-for-myself', with 'paths with wonderful paving' that satisfied his appetite for walking (KSB.6.68: 51). In a letter to his friend, Heinrich Köselitz, he wrote that to leave Genoa feels like 'leaving oneself behind' (KSB.8.1013: 285).

The Genoese palazzi left a strong impression on Nietzsche with their characterful display of human achievement and the noble pride of lives lived to the full. However, there was one palazzo that seems to have captivated him even more: the Palazzo Pitti in Florence, built 1458 (see Figure 2). This vast Renaissance palace, designed by Luca Fancelli, a pupil of Filippo Brunelleschi, struck Nietzsche as exuding a power of 'superhuman' proportions. He was introduced to the building by his colleague and mentor, Jacob Burckhardt, a historian of Italian Renaissance art and architecture whom Nietzsche met at the University of Basel. Nietzsche made extensive notes in his copies of Burckhardt's works. In *The Cicerone: An Art Guide to Painting in Italy for the Use of Travellers and Students* (1855/1879), Burckhardt argued that the power of a building lies in its material fabric, not in its symbolic meanings or decorative ornamentation, which distract from the overall impact. He further noted that, after the fifteenth century, the absence of ornament was celebrated for enhancing a building's sense of power. Nietzsche underlined these points in his copy, emphasising the words, 'detail', 'absence', 'impression of power'.

For those unfamiliar with Burckhardt's writings but more familiar with Nietzsche's, Burckhardt's description of the Palazzo Pitti may seem strikingly

Nietzschean. He described the palace as 'an image of the highest will power', the 'most ambitious' private building ever commissioned (1867/1987: 54, 14), and one created by 'superhuman beings' (1855: 175). Nietzsche shared Burckhardt's view that the Palazzo Pitti's power derived not from its sheer size or its elevated position on sloping ground, but from its 'rejection of all decoration', its simplicity of repetitive forms, and its avoidance of 'anything pleasing or delicate' (1855: 175). For Nietzsche, the Palazzo Pitti came to signify an antidote to the profound disappointment he felt over losing his former love for music. In a letter to Carl Fuchs, a musicologist and composer, Nietzsche wrote that the palazzo conveyed 'most intensely' the 'art of melody' (KSB.7.688: 177). I will revisit the significance of this building for Nietzsche in Chapter 4.

Although Nietzsche professed a deep affection for Genoa and a personal connection with its architecture, of all the places he visited or lived it was Turin that left the most profound impression on him. In Turin he both discovered and lost himself. Before visiting Turin, Nietzsche had written about the importance of finding

<u>'quiet and wide, expansive places for reflection—places with long, high-ceilinged arcades [...] buildings that give expression to the sublimity of contemplation and a stepping aside to take thought for oneself' (GS.280).</u>

Such places, he believed, encourage self-reflection and enable us to create in harmony with our instinctual needs. Turin seemed to provide precisely this environment. He wrote effusively about the city's architecture, exclaiming to his friend Köselitz, 'This really is the city I need! What a dignified and serious city', marked by 'one commanding taste everywhere, that of court and nobility. An aristocratic calm is preserved in everything'. He admired the city's 'unity of taste' that filters down even to its colours, for the 'whole city is yellow or red-brown' (KSB.8.1013: 285). To his mother, he described Turin as 'the only city I like living in', with its 'magnificent, spacious portici, colonnades and hallways' that ran alongside the main streets and connected squares, extending '10,020 metres' throughout the city (KSB.8.1018: 293). It is 'paradise for the feet!' (KSB.8.1016: 292).

Nietzsche resided at Via Carlo Alberto 6, in an apartment near the top of the Galleria Subalpina, an elegant shopping arcade inspired by the Parisian arcades and built in 1873–4 by Pietro Carrera (Figure 1). The Galleria, similar in style to Milan's Galleria Vittorio Emanuele II, combined Renaissance and Baroque elements, featuring marble pillars and a vaulted roof of wrought iron and glass. The building is approximately 50 metres long, 14 metres wide, and 18 metres high, with a balcony running along its perimeter. Nietzsche described his apartment to Köselitz as 'a splendid high room' and remarked that when he stepped out, he looked down into 'the most beautiful and elegant space of its kind that I know of' (KSB.8[1192]: 528). From outside his apartment, he enjoyed

Figure 1 Galleria Subalpina, Turin (built 1873–74, Pietro Carrera). Interior. Looking towards Nietzsche's apartment. Author's photograph.

views into the Galleria, including his favourite café, *Caffee Baratti & Milano*, and to the Piazza Carlo Alberto in the opposite direction.

A walk from Nietzsche's apartment through the Galleria Subalpina led him to Piazza Castello and the Palazzo Madama, which he affectionately referred to as 'my palazzo'. Reflecting on this building, Nietzsche remarked, 'We'll have to supply the *madama* ourselves—: it can remain exactly as it is, by far the most picturesque kind of grand castle, especially its stairwell' (KSB.8.1227: 565). The palazzo is a curious hybrid of medieval fortified castle and Baroque palace, embodying a union of opposites—a symbolic theme Nietzsche was fond of, especially in his quest for the creative fusion of the Apollonian and Dionysian. The site originally served as a Roman gate, remnants of which are still visible, before it was developed into a fortified castle in the late thirteenth century by the Savoia-Acaja, a branch of the House of Savoy. In the seventeenth century, it was partially remodelled into a residential palace by members of the Savoy family—notably Christine Marie of France and Marie-Jeanne-Baptiste of Savoy-Nemours. They commissioned the Sicilian architect Filippo Juvarra to enhance the site with a palace of white stone, though only the façade was completed (1718–21). This part of the building houses the impressive double stairwell Nietzsche admired, but he would have most often seen the building from its castle-side, as he exited the Galleria Subalpina onto Via Po.

A ten-minute walk along cobbled streets from Nietzsche's apartment brought him to a building with which he felt the deepest connection, one that he identified with both personally and in relation to his creative works: the Mole Antonelliana (see Figure 3). This structure, built between 1863 and 1889 by Italian architect, Alessandro Antonelli, became a symbol for Nietzsche. He described it as

'the greatest work of genius ever built out of an absolute instinct for height—suggestive of nothing so much as my Zarathustra.

I have christened it "Ecce Homo" and mentally surrounded it with an immense open space' (KSB.8.1227: 565). Nietzsche imagined the Mole standing isolated, apart from other buildings, much like how, as a boy, he wished for the 'high, venerable city church' of St. Wenzel in Naumburg to be surrounded by empty space, unobstructed by lesser structures.

Named after its architect, Antonelli (1798–1888), the Mole was initially intended to function as a synagogue for Turin, the capital of the newly unified Italian state. However, it was never used for this purpose, partly due to the departure of many Jewish residents to Florence when it became the capital in 1864. Escalating costs and delayed timelines—driven by Antonelli's ambition to make the Mole ever taller—also forced his clients to withdraw from the project. Upon its completion, the Mole stood nearly 170 metres high, 46 metres taller than originally planned. At that time, it was the tallest unreinforced brick building in Europe.

Nietzsche's productivity abruptly ended in Turin when he collapsed in a street or palazzo in late December 1888 or early January 1889, depending on which account you read. According to reports, upon witnessing a coachman cruelly whipping his horse, Nietzsche threw his arms around the animal's neck, sobbing uncontrollably, before collapsing. This incident marked the onset of a mental breakdown that incapacitated him for the rest of his life, until his death in 1900. While this event has gained legendary status, little attention has been given to the significance of the Mole Antonelliana for Nietzsche's personal life and his philosophical vision, or to his identification with the building in the days leading up to his collapse. In Chapter 4, I delve into the relevance of this building for Nietzsche. After his collapse, in his final letter, written on 6 January 1889, Nietzsche wrote to Jacob Burckhardt, suggesting that he, Nietzsche, had once been Antonelli, the architect, and recommending that Burckhardt visit Turin to see this building for himself (KSB.8.1256: 579).

Following his collapse, Nietzsche spent a year in an asylum in Jena before moving to Naumburg, where his mother cared for him. After her death in April 1897, his sister Elisabeth took over both his care and stewardship of his intellectual legacy. She relocated Nietzsche and his archive of unpublished works to a three-storey redbrick house called Villa Silberblick situated on the outskirts of Weimar at Luisenstraße 30 (now, Humboldtstraße 36). Elisabeth noted how pleased Nietzsche was with the house 'from the first moment he entered the lonely house' (Cohn and Förster-Nietzsche, 1931: 156). She recounted that, upon his arrival, Nietzsche carefully examined the decor, wandering the house without needing support, saying always 'Palazzo, palazzo' (Kessler, 2011: 187). Elisabeth described how the relationships between height and light, with the high ceilings, and 'beautiful view' of 'the wide horizon', had a therapeutic effect on him, allowing him to walk unaided, speak again, and even read and comment on what he had read (Förster-Nietzsche, 1914: 544).

On 25 August 1900, Nietzsche died in Villa Silberblick. Elisabeth commissioned Belgian designer and architect Henry van de Velde to redesign the building in a manner befitting Nietzsche's philosophy. In Chapter 5, I examine van de Velde's design, along with several other buildings created to honour Nietzsche's philosophical vision, to assess how they interpreted the spatial representation of his ideas.

This chapter has introduced some of the buildings and places that captured Nietzsche's attention, from his first home, which left an indelible mark on him— 'engraved', as he remarked, 'in his soul'—to the final building he described, the Mole Antonelliana, with which he felt intimately identified. I have also begun to outline some of Nietzsche's key ideas for understanding his experiences of architecture, along with the principles that shaped his attraction to certain buildings. These include the idea of architecture as a spatial manifestation of the will to power; the transformative power of architecture on individuals, groups, and entire cultures; the need to balance rationalised structures with instinctual forms (expressed in Nietzsche's terms as the creative interplay between Apollonian and Dionysian elements); the intimate relationship between architectural design and our sense of feeling embodied or disembodied, connected or alienated from place; and the drive to cultivate our creative talents by pushing the boundaries of innovation and achievement (which Nietzsche called a desire for the heights or height instinct). These themes provide a framework for considering what a 'Nietzschean architecture' might entail, and in the following chapters I will delve deeper into these concepts to explore how the design features of some of the buildings discussed here helped Nietzsche develop some of his most significant philosophical ideas.

CHAPTER 3

Decadent modern architecture

Amassed rather than *assembled*'

Nietzsche was both a fiercely critical thinker and a philosopher who affirmed and constructed new values. He advocated for a 'revaluation of values', encouraging a positive approach to life by discarding false and restrictive ideals that have constrained our freedom—such as idealised notions of permanence, eternal truths, and transcendental values. For Nietzsche, the highest value is living well, which requires us to assert and exercise our own creative powers. Through this, we can generate fresh and imaginative designs that elevate the aspirations of individuals, communities, and entire cultures. However, Nietzsche believed that modern European culture had been corrupted by an all-pervading will to truth, which resulted in sterile, decadent values and uninspiring cultural products.

This chapter and the following one explore Nietzsche's dual role as critic and visionary in response to modern architectural design. This chapter will address his critique of modern German architecture of his day, while Chapter 4 will evaluate his proposals for more relevant, sustainable, and meaningful designs for contemporary life.

Last men and cultivated philistines: problems of excessive knowledge and its weak application

Nietzsche's positive vision of life is embodied in the figure of the 'Übermensch', or superman, while his critique of modern culture is represented by the opposing figure of the last man, or 'Letzter Mensch'. In *Thus Spoke Zarathustra* (1883–5), the last man is described as a mediocre individual who cannot affirm life. Lacking ambition, the last man avoids risk and innovation, driven by a will to truth rather than a will to power. This passive approach to life prioritises comfort and certainty, primarily achieved through the accumulation of knowledge. Nietzsche believed that nineteenth-century European culture was drifting towards the realisation of the last man, reflecting the idea that life's ultimate goal had already been reached through historical progress and the pursuit of reason. The last man is content because he believes he possesses complete self-knowledge and an understanding of everything that has ever happened, leaving nothing more to strive for. He gathers knowledge for its own sake but lacks the wisdom to apply it meaningfully in the present, preventing him from living creatively and effectively. Zarathustra remarks that the last men 'blink' frequently, as if afflicted by a neurotic twitch, symptomatic of their inability to manage their instinctual nature and allow the Dionysian impulses of life to express themselves naturally.

A decade before introducing the last man, Nietzsche discussed a similar figure called the 'cultivated philistine'. This figure serves as a precursor to the last man, embodying the antithesis of those 'who are powerful and creative'. Both figures share a passive attitude towards life, rooted in the belief that there is no need to seek further because everything meaningful has already been discovered and can be learnt by emulating other cultivated individuals (UM.I.2). Nietzsche used an architectural analogy to illustrate the deluded thinking of the cultivated philistine. The philistine insists there is no need to search for a new foundation upon which 'the German spirit might erect its house', claiming instead that 'not only is the foundation [already] there, but the entire edifice already stands erected upon it—we ourselves are this edifice'. Nietzsche continued: 'Saying this, the philistine lays his hand on his own brow' (UM.I.2).

Nietzsche employed additional architectural metaphors to critique the modern mindset, including a metaphorical structure constructed by the cultivated philistine in the name of German culture, which I will survey at the end of this chapter.

<u>According to Nietzsche, modern Germans are so burdened by facts and knowledge that they relate to themselves in abstract terms, as if disembodied and disconnected from the sensual and immediate qualities of their natural and built environments.</u>

He described their mindset as 'essentially inward', comparing the average modern person to a 'walking encyclopaedia', labelled by a bookbinder as a 'Handbook of Inward Cultivation for Outward Barbarians' (UM.II.4). Nietzsche regarded modern German culture as a mere repository of facts from past cultures, failing to foster great art and architecture. People tended, he thought, to take pride in accumulating even more information in ever-greater forensic detail and nuance, widening the gap between their inner and outer worlds by prioritising rationality over instinct, further desensitising themselves to their material surroundings.

This disconnection is evident in what Nietzsche called the 'chaotic mishmash of all styles' in modern German society. He argued that whenever a German person looks at 'their room, and their house' or 'walks through the streets of their cities', they are confronted by the 'grotesque juxtaposition and jumbling of all possible styles'. Germans surround themselves with a 'carnival motley' of forms, colours, and products from all ages and cultures, leading to a jumbled, grotesque aesthetic (UM.I:1). In an unpublished note from 1873, Nietzsche criticised the absence of style in 'dwellings, rooms', 'theatres', and 'museums', calling them 'proof of the most absolute absence of style'. He argued that these structures have clearly been *amassed* rather than *assembled* (KSA.14.161: 60; KSA.7.29[58]: 653). Zarathustra, Nietzsche's fictional spokesperson, echoes these critiques. Upon seeing a row of newly built houses, he asks 'What do these houses mean?' noting that 'no great soul put them up as its image!'. He continues,

> Did a silly child perhaps take them out of its toy-box? If only another child would put them back into its box! And these sitting rooms and bedrooms: are *men* able to go in and out of them? They seem to have been made for dolls.

Zarathustra longs to return to the high vistas of his mountain cave, where 'I shall no longer have to stoop *before the small men!*' (Z.III.5[1]: 187).

Historicism and style-revivalism: the problem of relying on others for inspiration

Nietzsche's critique can be seen as a response to the historicism and style-revivalism that were popular in Germany at the time. In the latter half of the nineteenth century, Germany was a global industrial leader in science, technology, and commerce. After receiving substantial war reparations from the Franco-Prussian war (1870–1) and its subsequent unification into the German Empire, the nation experienced economic prosperity, leading to increased housing developments and a national drive to improve the aesthetic quality of mass-produced goods, art, and architecture. This period saw green fields transformed into residential areas, often featuring large buildings with four to six storeys and richly decorated façades in various revivalist styles.

For Nietzsche, these architectural designs exemplified the deeper cultural issue: the failure to inspire or engage the imagination, relying instead on imitations of historical styles that reflected a lack of inventive and creative spirit. He argued that the ailing German spirit revealed itself in its tendency to emulate ideas of greatness from the past. As long as the nation remained committed to this approach, it stifled the potential for more innovative, experimental designs that could better address its contemporary needs. This mindset fostered a superficial pretence of greatness, driven by appearance rather than substance. 'Just take a stroll through any German city' he wrote, 'everything is colourless, worn out, badly copied, slipshod; everyone does as they like' but without care or thought, driven by 'the universal addiction to comfort' (UM.II.4).

In one of Nietzsche's most quoted remarks about architecture, he laments, 'we no longer understand architecture', and 'we have lost touch with the symbolism of lines and figures'. He asks, 'What is the beauty of a building to us now?—it is "masklike"' (HHI.218).

Façades adorned with a mishmash of historical styles can be seen as mask-like, as Nietzsche believed they presented only a caricature of cultural values. The symbolism in their lines and figures seems purely for display, failing to engage the viewer beyond surface-level impressions.

Nietzsche's perspective on this matter was probably shaped by Gottfried Semper, whom Nietzsche regarded as 'the most significant living architect' (I examine their relationship in Chapter 5). Semper was concerned about the late nineteenth-century academic trend of meticulously analysing and cataloguing historical architectural styles. He argued that this abundance of research had led to confusion among contemporary architects, who were left uncertain about which style to emulate in their own work. Semper wrote,

> Just as the abundance of technical means is an embarrassment to us, even more so are we perplexed by the immense mass of historical knowledge, which increases daily. Every trend of taste is familiar to us, from the times of the Assyrian and Egyptian styles to the age of Louis XVI and beyond. We can do everything; we know everything except ourselves!
> (Semper in Herrmann, 1981: MS. 88, fol. 34)

Semper described replicas of past architectural styles as 'historical treatises in stone' and 'eerie phantasmagorias' (Semper in Herrmann, 1981: MS. 25, fol. 5). Mirroring Nietzsche's complaint, Semper noted that such historicist designs revealed 'the dire poverty of our own ideas and dependence on those of others' (MS. 25, fol. 258). He similarly lamented that in Germany, 'architecture as an art has been confined to a beautiful façade, planted there without any attempt at integration' (MS. 25, fol. 53).

Nietzsche argued that revivalist vernacular architecture encouraged people to hide behind façades, both psychologically and architecturally. These styles direct a person's attention away from the organic needs of everyday life and towards abstract ideals, fostering the erroneous belief that such buildings are beneficial. This perpetuates the cycle of constructing buildings that prioritise functionality and cost-effectiveness, which, at best, captivate us with superficial sentimental charm and visual spectacle, or, at worst, create a sense of alienation from ourselves, our surroundings, and one another.

In this context, buildings become objects to critique and contemplate from a distance, rather than spaces that help people connect with themselves and their environments. Instead of fostering introspection, these buildings stand as obstacles to self-awareness. They are far from the 'quiet' buildings that 'step aside' to allow for self-reflection, that Nietzsche described (GS.280). By referencing past stylistic features, such buildings distract and invite people to decode their symbolism. Nietzsche sought a cleansing of architecture, advocating designs that do not draw undue attention to themselves with arbitrary 'chatter'. He urged us to 'avoid today' the 'noise', 'chatter', and 'junk of the marketplace', and instead seek 'quiet places' where 'we can speak without speaking *out loud*' and do so unobserved (GM.III.8).

A Gothic cathedral might be seen as particularly problematic in this context, with its intricate details often depicting religious iconography intended to instruct worshippers visually in the divine 'truths' of scripture. However, any building with a distinctive historical style tends to impose the ideals, values, and principles of a bygone era—ideals that may not be especially relevant or useful for the creative lives of people today.

The need for a unifying instinct

Germany, as Nietzsche noted, suffered from a lack of 'unifying instinct'. Without this, cultural accomplishments become fragmented and disordered, reflected in its architecture as a chaotic assembly of fanciful ideas and a mishmash of styles. I revisit this important notion in Chapter 4, where I explain its role in the relationship between the will to power and architecture. As I show, the will to power serves as the 'central organizing power' (BGE.242), uniting all instincts (KSA.12.9[166]: 433, 435).

A few months after Nietzsche published the first two of his *Untimely Meditations* or *Unfashionable Observations* (1873–6/2001), critiquing German culture, he wrote to his friend, Erwin Rohde: 'In the meantime, I have chosen Rothenburg ob der Tauber as my private castle and hermitage; I want to visit in the summer. At least things there are still German, in the old-fashioned way', unlike modern German cities, which 'I hate' for being 'characterless', 'mixed', and lacking 'wholeness' (BVN.364: 226–7). Nietzsche appears to distinguish between 'old German' styles and contemporary architecture, raising the question of whether he favoured traditional Germanic architectural customs over radically 'new' designs detached from historical roots. The answer, as I will further elaborate, is that Nietzsche sought to revive the creative spirit that had produced the great architectural feats of history, but in a way that responded to the present needs of society. He envisioned an architecture that, while looking towards the future and embracing new horizons, remains recognisable and meaningful to people today. This idea is exemplified in his admiration for the Genoese Baroque palazzi, which, to Nietzsche, embodied a 'thirst for something new', while also honouring the past by establishing 'a new world alongside the old' (GS.291). The creators of these structures were grounded in the material realities of their time and sought to enrich their world by shaping it with their vision, rather than abandoning it entirely to create something nonsensical and uninspiring to others.

Architectural analogies of a declining culture

Nietzsche imagined a variety of buildings, each embodying distinctive problems that reflected his broader critique of modern European culture, particularly German culture. Individually and collectively, these structures represent the antithesis of his creative philosophy. By examining them, we gain a clearer understanding of Nietzsche's vision for a more constructive approach to architectural design—one that aligns with individual and cultural needs. The flawed buildings he described are inhabited or constructed by individuals who personify the ailing modern mindset, such as the cultivated philistine (modelled on the theological writer David Strauss) and Wagner, whom Nietzsche referred to as the *'modern artist par excellence'* (CW.I.5).

Earlier, I mentioned Zarathustra's frustration at trying to enter houses in a modern city. They were too small and restrictive, forcing him to stoop. Later in his travels, he observes that even the most cultured individuals, the 'higher men', lack the necessary stature. He subsequently retreats to his mountain cave, waiting for those capable of ascending to his lofty terrain—for 'those who are higher, stronger, more victorious, and more joyful, such as are built right-angled in body and soul' (Z.IV.11: 294). Inhabitants of stunted buildings in modern cities are unlikely to venture far from their houses, content to remain in their cramped interiors. These houses are designed by and for people with stunted ambition. They subsequently constrain Zarathustra's movements and cramp his style. For Zarathustra, these modern homes imprison their residents like cells or mausoleums: a 'completely modern person who wants to build themselves a house' feels just the same as a person who wants 'to entomb their living body in a mausoleum' (HH1.22).

Nietzsche used the labyrinth as another architectural metaphor, symbolising a structure that restricts movement and imprisons people within its walls. However, while labyrinthine pathways can constrict and bewilder, they can also reveal new directions and possibilities. Nietzsche regarded the labyrinth in both positive and negative terms. On the one hand, he envisioned it as a vast, intimate place where one can withdraw for self-reflection and unapologetically be oneself, 'where no tyranny can penetrate' (UM.III.3). In this respect, it resembles the empty spaces Nietzsche advocates for escaping the chaos of city life and taking time to reflect. The labyrinth is a place of 'daring insights' (EH.III.3), where the 'most intelligent humans, as the *strongest*, find their happiness' (AC.57). On the other hand, it is a dangerous place where many 'find their destruction' (AC.57). It is a place to 'bless', even if one 'almost perishes' there, because without this struggle, one 'cannot create' one only 'dies' (KSA.5[1]225: 213).

Moreover, entering a labyrinth makes a person invisible to others, so if they become 'lost, lonely', or are 'torn apart piece by piece by some cave minotaur of conscience', nobody will witness 'how and where' it happens (BGE.29), leaving little hope of rescue. The labyrinth is dangerous because it forces you to question yourself and the ideas discovered within. The insights it offers can induce loneliness, as they are often 'uncommunicative and reluctant' and 'blow cold air at every passerby' (BGE.289). Nietzsche also likened the modern mindset to a labyrinth. To retreat inwardly into one's own labyrinth, he asserted, is the 'greatest danger' because we need to 'live externally' and 'be seen' by others (UM.III.3). Labyrinths encourage withdrawal from the material world, and this is a significant problem for modern Germans. Nietzsche asserted that

if modern individuals were not too cowardly to design architecture that reflects their inner selves, it would be 'a labyrinth' (D.169).

Labyrinths can be rewarding places of creative insight, reflection, and discovery, but they also have the potential to mislead, confuse, and alienate. The outcome for Nietzsche, I think, depends on how one navigates its complex architecture. Nietzsche berated the modern mindset for embracing a will to truth, which fixates on the accumulation of facts, information, and abstract ideas. A modern labyrinth can therefore be regarded as a repository of ideas—a maze of causal connections, overly complex passages, and concealed chambers—into which we are systematically lured by educational and cultural institutions, only to end up trapped, lost, and thwarted by dead ends.

Nietzsche's remedy to this modern labyrinth, as I will further explore, is to approach it with a will to power. This will assigns to instincts their proper 'way and direction', giving us the confidence to explore the labyrinth independently and uncover insights relevant to our own experiences. It reawakens our somatic responses, enabling us to navigate its twists and turns with greater instinct and intuition.

The rest of this chapter examines two buildings—one real, one imaginary—that reflect Nietzsche's criticisms of modern German culture. The first is Richard

Wagner's Festspielhaus in Bayreuth, a place dedicated to Wagner's music, from which Nietzsche fled in horror during its inaugural concert. He would later describe Wagner as the 'best practised guide for the labyrinth of the modern soul' (CW.7). However, this does not imply that Wagner helps people find their way through the labyrinth; instead, he lures them into its most constricting places to play a 'game of hide-and-seek among a hundred symbols' (CW.10). The second building I consider is Nietzsche's analogy of David Strauss's house, the house of the cultivated philistine, and 'labyrinth to all who are circumspect and lost [...]' (UM.I.2).

Disembodied architecture, tricks, and superficial effects: Wagner's Festspielhaus in Bayreuth

Looking back on his relationship with Wagner, Nietzsche remarked, 'I needed Wagner to get free from the Germans' with their overly rational mindset. However, he added, 'Wagner is the counter-poison to everything German par excellence—still poison. I do not dispute it' (EH.II.6). Wagner remained for Nietzsche a personification of the failure of modern German culture, particularly in Wagner's desire for the sublime to make him feel alive. In Nietzsche's view, Wagner and his followers avoided self-reflection, preferring to be overwhelmed by superficial effects, dramatic flourishes, and theatrical posturing—all of which, Wagner's music provided in abundance (CW.6).

Central to Wagner's artistic failure, according to Nietzsche, was his lack of 'rhythmic feeling' and 'organizing power'. This shortcoming inhibited his ability to create a cohesive, unified style that could inspire creativity in others. While Nietzsche acknowledged Wagner's ability to master 'microscopic features of the soul', he criticised Wagner for inventing 'little unities', which he would then 'animate, inflate, and make visible'. But in doing so, Nietzsche argued, Wagner exhausted his artistic potential, resulting in a 'complete degeneration' of 'rhythmical feeling', with '*chaos* in place of rhythm' (CW.7; CW.Postscript).

Wagner's Festspielhaus, built to showcase his performances, was described by Wagner as close to realising his vision of an 'ideal' architectural structure for his art (Wagner, 1873). As such, the Festspielhaus can be regarded as emblematic of Wagner's creative instincts, and, by extension, the deeper issues Nietzsche sought to address. Although Nietzsche did not discuss the design of Wagner's Festspielhaus beyond its orchestra pit, several features of the building resonate with Nietzsche's broader criticisms of Wagner and modern decadence.

The Festspielhaus was, in part, a distorted adaptation of Gottfried Semper's earlier design for a theatre for Wagner's music in Munich, a project that was never realised. According to Semper's son, Manfred, Semper felt insulted by Wagner's decision to incorporate features of his design without permission (M. Semper, 1906: 102). Wagner enlisted another architect, Otto Brückwald, to execute the design, which, as Wagner later confessed to Semper, was inferior to the original, describing it as 'clumsy and tasteless' (Habel, 1970: 314). Architectural theorist Fritz Neumeyer critiqued the Festspielhaus, noting that from an architectural point of view, there is hardly anything uplifting to say about it, because nothing really fits together. Even the untrained eye does not miss the blatant lack of relationship between its components (Neumeyer, 2001/2004: 117). The building could be said to express the 'modern carnival motley' that so troubled Nietzsche, a 'chaotic mishmash of all styles' (UM.I.1). Neumeyer further described the Festspielhaus as an 'awkward mix' that is 'stubborn' and 'pompous', more akin to a factory, purpose-built agricultural or industrial building than a theatre. In fact, it even avoided bombing during World War II, because allied pilots mistook it for a brewery (2001/2004: 117).

Nietzsche argued that while Wagner's artistry may allure with its fleeting effects, it ultimately deceives by offering only an 'imitation of greatness'. Wagner thus reinforces the problematic split in the modern mindset, and his Festspielhaus symbolises this split with its incongruous combination of a plain, bare exterior and the grandiosity of the spectacle inside. Wagner paid little attention to the exterior design, instead investing his resources in stage machinery and scenery to ensure the interior reflected his vision of the 'ideal inner work of art—*perfect* in every way'. The simple exterior of timber and brick was meant to be a 'humble shell', designed only to be sturdy enough to 'prevent it from collapsing' (Baker, 1998: 60). The contrasting treatment of the exterior and interior reflects a lack of creative balance between Apollonian restraint and Dionysian exuberance, with the exterior adhering to functional Apollonian principles and the interior giving the Dionysian free rein.

Initially, Nietzsche was enthusiastic about the Festspielhaus, from its design phase to the laying of its foundation stone, but his feelings drastically changed when the theatre opened in the summer of 1876. In an unpublished note, he reflects: 'My mistake was to come to Bayreuth with an ideal. I was forced to experience the bitterest disappointment. The excess of ugliness, distortion, and overexcitement repulsed me vehemently' (KSA.8.30[1]: 522). He later described his profound alienation: 'Not one monstrosity is lacking' (EH.VI.HH.2). For Nietzsche, Wagner had created a grandiose spectacle of delusion. He wrote, the theatre 'offers us a magnifying glass: you look through it and cannot believe your eyes—everything becomes big, *even Wagner*' (CW.3).

A key feature of the Festspielhaus that upset Nietzsche was the sunken orchestra pit, adapted by Brückwald from Semper's Munich design. This innovation contributed to Nietzsche's harsh assessment of Wagner as a mere 'master of hypnotic tricks' (CW.5). The hidden orchestra was designed to make the music seem as if it emanated from another world, a 'mystical chasm' (Baker, 1998: 262; Wagner, 1873), heightening the illusion that the audience was being transported to a metaphysical realm. This effect was further amplified by another feature borrowed from Semper: the linear seating arrangement. This set-up provided an uninterrupted view of the stage, making the actors appear much closer and imbuing them with an almost 'superhuman stature' to reinforce the other-worldly experience Wagner sought to create (Baker, 1998: 262; Wagner, 1873).

Wagner's ideal architecture was an invisible architecture, and this was problematic for Nietzsche. It was not simply the various tricks enabled by such an architecture that concerned Nietzsche, but the sense of disembodiment they fostered. Invisible architecture can be bewildering and disorientating, lacking the solidity needed to ground us and to enable us to experience ourselves safely in place. The absence of a tangible structure gives Dionysian forces an unchecked freedom, leading to the obliteration and dissolution of Apollonian order and distinctive form.

Architecture for the Cultivated Philistine

Nietzsche harboured a deep contempt for the optimistic complacency of the cultivated philistine, of individuals who mistakenly fancied themselves as highly cultured. Their lack of self-awareness and naïve misunderstanding stemmed from the fact that they continually encountered others of the 'same type' and that 'all public institutions' of 'schooling, education, and art' were organised according to their shallow notion of 'cultivatedness'. This reinforced their delusional 'triumphant feeling of being the worthy representative of present-day German culture' (UM.I.2). The homogeneity among 'cultivated' individuals created the erroneous assumption that German culture had a unified style, but Nietzsche argued that homogeneity is not the same as unity of style. The cultivated philistine only recognised the '"German culture" he has patented', rejecting anything that does not align with his ideals.

<u>Nietzsche believed that a truly cultured person acts in opposition to modern cultural institutions.</u>

Nietzsche expanded on his critique of the cultivated philistine by referring to the work of David Strauss, who was quickly becoming a national trendsetter of culture and taste. In his book, *The Old Faith and the New* (1872), Strauss presented himself as a freethinker and founder of a new kind of humanistic religion. While the book was widely praised for its approach, Nietzsche criticised its content and style, viewing it as a presumptuous catalogue of vague abstractions, mixed metaphors, and sloppy, sentimental prose. For Nietzsche, this revealed the failure of contemporary Germans to recognise and appreciate style as a fundamental element of culture, allowing themselves to be hoodwinked into adopting an easy approach to life.

Instead of discovering life through creative power and artistic struggle, as Nietzsche had advocated, Strauss reduced it to the comforts of a cultivated existence, which Nietzsche described as an 'ever-growing compendium of scholarly opinions about art, literature, and philosophy' (UM.I.8). Nietzsche also condemned Strauss for his careless and cowardly attempts to combine scientific materialism with religious faith, as though by sleight of hand. Rather than retreating into metaphysical comforts, Nietzsche argued that Strauss should have the courage to tell his readers that life is indifferent. Nietzsche further accused Strauss of softening the harsh realities of the mechanistic worldview, likening him to a 'metaphysical architect'.

Nietzsche developed this analogy by comparing Strauss's role as a cultivated philistine to a reckless architect who is able only to construct a flawed building with faulty design and unstable engineering:

> Even once this all-important task is accomplished and the edifice itself has been erected in harmonious proportions, there is still much left to be done: how many minor defects must be corrected, how many gaps filled; here and there provisional partitions or scaffolds have had to suffice for the time being; everywhere you turn there is dust and rubble, and wherever you look you see the signs of problems and of ongoing labour. The house as a whole is still uninhabitable and unhomey; all the walls are naked, and the wind whips through the open windows.
>
> (UM.I.9)

Nietzsche suggested it was pointless to question whether Strauss had the 'capacity to build his house', or the necessary 'artistic power' and 'vision to create a totality'. Strauss, he argued, followed the scholarly conventions of his time by *assembling* his edifice 'out of bits and pieces', trusting that these fragments 'have a coherence unto themselves', and thereby confusing logic with 'artistic coherence' (UM.I.9).

Nietzsche examined the interior of Strauss's metaphorical house, likening its rooms to sections of Strauss's book. As a cultivated philistine with a 'cramped and dried up soul' and intense 'scholarly needs', Strauss has constructed something closer to a 'garden house' or pavilion, rather than a 'temple' or 'residence'. This structure emphasises aesthetic effects over coordinated design and sound engineering (UM.I.10; 9). Although the house's inhabitants appear to enjoy its comfortable furnishings, the building itself is defective, unfinished, and riddled with gaps and holes, leaving it exposed to subsidence and erosion from harsh weather. The discrepancy between its structural integrity and the comfort its residents experience suggests only those in a state of delusion could live there.

Nietzsche's tour of the garden house begins in the 'gloom' of its 'theological catacombs', furnished with 'convoluted and Baroque ornamentation'. This contrasts starkly with the next room—a brightly lit hall, illuminated by artificial light, where 'rationality' reigns. The walls are adorned with celestial charts and mathematical tables, and the room is filled with scientific instruments, cabinets of skeletons, stuffed apes, and anatomical specimens. Nietzsche observed that, upon entering, we feel 'genuinely happy' immersed in the 'total comfort of those who dwell' here. Residents are 'engrossed in their newspapers and mundane political discussions'. He noted how quickly they can recite the public opinions of the day, suggesting their minds are filled with shallow thoughts.

Finally, Strauss attempted to 'convince us of the classical taste' of the house's residents, and a 'brief visit to the library and the music room confirms our expectations' that 'only the best books line the shelves, and only the most celebrated compositions are on the music stands'. The 'owner of this garden house praises himself and expresses the opinion that anyone who is not happy here is beyond help and not ripe for his standpoint' (UM.I.9).

This chapter explored Nietzsche's critique of the modern architecture of his day as symptomatic of a broader cultural decay—a sign of a culture overwhelmed by knowledge but lacking purpose. He regarded the designs of contemporary German buildings as sterile, derivative, and uninspiring, and completely at odds with the vibrant creativity he valued. He condemned the chaotic revivalist styles of his time as a 'mishmash' of outmoded forms and passive imitations that prioritised comfort over innovation.

Nietzsche employed architectural metaphors to discuss representative figures of contemporary culture as he saw it, like the 'cultivated philistine', whose disjointed and fragmented creations resemble poorly designed, unstable houses. He extended his criticisms to Richard Wagner, accusing Wagner of leading audiences astray and into a symbolic labyrinth to play a 'game of hide-and-seek among a hundred symbols'—an indictment that also targets the design of Wagner's Bayreuth Festspielhaus.

Nietzsche called for architecture to be grounded in the creative will to power, which unites instinct to produce meaningful, original designs. In contrast, he regarded the dependence on historical styles as a mask, beneath which hides a stagnating culture lacking in originality. Ultimately, Nietzsche sought architecture that fosters introspection and aligns with the needs of individuals and society to provoke renewal and vitality. In the next chapter, I explore Nietzsche's positive view of architecture in greater depth to understand how he envisioned the potential of architecture to empower individuals, groups, and cultures.

CHAPTER 4

The will to power as a will to build

This chapter presents Nietzsche's positive approach to architecture, which fosters creativity and cultural achievement through the exercise of the will to power. In doing so, I will revisit some of the buildings described in Chapter 2 that Nietzsche admired and celebrated.

Nietzsche asserted that the 'one thing needful' is 'to give style to one's character'. He was critical of modern German architecture for consistently failing to achieve this. Rather than succeeding to develop an organic style of its own, it borrowed ideas and ideals from other eras, places, and peoples, resulting in a mere caricature of style. Nietzsche thought that modern Germany championed a fragmented disarray of styles, assembled from other cultures, driven by the rationalised judgements of its so-called 'educational' institutions and 'cultivated' leaders. As an expression of this cultural outlook, German architecture became overly stylised and lacked an organic style of its own. The German people ought to have created a unified and distinctive style of their own, an architecture that celebrated and nurtured their vitality. In other words, they needed to give style to their character by moving away from a desire simply to gather and scrutinise past discoveries and engage themselves instead in an open-ended search for a style that addressed their specific needs.

<u>Nietzsche urged us all to abandon the 'comfortable pastime of finding' and instead embrace 'the restless creative spirit' of searching, as it is the search that 'animates the artist' (UM.I.2).</u>

To give style to one's character means to seek only what is necessary for creative development, while avoiding distractions and needless 'chatter' (GM.III.8). By exercising the will to power, architects and artists can identify and harness what is necessary for themselves, as well as their communities and the people they design for.

Will to power

In earlier chapters, I discussed the will to power as the 'central organising power' that channels our instincts, exploiting the tensions between them to maximise our creative potential. Artists continuously exercise their will to power, shaping and reshaping themselves as creative individuals. Nietzsche emphasised that 'one is *fruitful* at the cost of being rich in contradictions', and that 'one remains *young* only on condition the soul does not relax, does not long for peace' (TI.V.3:66). Those with the mental strength to withstand the struggle of competing perspectives, while preventing any one view from becoming habitual or dominant, can tap into their instinctual energies to revitalise their ideas and reawaken their somatic engagement with things. In doing so, they become more self-aware, resourceful, and 'alive'.

In this scenario, the problematic dualism Nietzsche identified at the core of modern culture—where abstract thought is collectively prioritised over instinctual engagement with the material world—would be overcome. Similarly, the suppression of Dionysian approaches to life by Apollonian ones would be removed, allowing for a healthier dialogue between the two.

Nietzsche underscored the importance of *living* life, rather than attempting to understand it through abstract formulas. Life is experienced and embodied through ceaseless activity. In this sense, the will to power represents the fundamental law of life:

> Our entire instinctual life [is] the development and ramification of *one* basic form of will—as will to power ... [O]ne [can] trace all organic functions back to this will to power and also find in it the solution to the problem of procreation and nourishment.
>
> (BGE.36; cf.259)

The will to power allows us to live fuller, richer lives. However, as I have intimated, Nietzsche recognised that this is no easy feat. Most people will fail to meet the demands it places on us, and will instead choose a more passive existence, following the 'herd' and adhering to a will to truth. While the will to power demands heroism, strength, and conscious affirmation, the will to truth feeds off unconscious submission, weakness of will, and supressed creativity. Those who prefer comfort, peace, and security within a community of accepted truths and common values, over the tension, strife, and uncertainty that lead to creative innovation, may experience occasional happiness but will never achieve satisfaction (KSA.13:11[75]: 37–8). As Nietzsche suggested, such individuals 'become nothing;' they do not *live* but abstract themselves from life (HHI.626).

Exercising the will to power means giving style to one's character, which involves continual self-scrutiny to ascertain 'what is necessary in things' and to 'take delight' in the necessities one imposes on oneself (GS.276,335; TI.IX.9: 93). This requires, Nietzsche wrote, 'the will to economy' (AC.Foreword). However, maintaining such concentration is difficult and relatively hopeless for those with a weak will, who prefer the decadent comforts of modern life. Such self-scrutiny demands deep-seated honesty, a robust intellectual conscience, and daily practice (GS.290; HHI.163).

A life shaped by the will to power involves intensive self-mastery and the adoption of self-defined values, which Nietzsche refers to as 'master morality'. This stands in stark contrast to a life dominated by 'slave morality', where one cannot master instincts and seeks a negative sense of power by adopting values imposed by others. Nietzsche's understanding of morality diverges radically from deontological frameworks, such as Immanuel Kant's notion of a universal, a priori rational law that dictates how we ought to act. For Nietzsche, 'there are no moral phenomena at all, only moral interpretations of phenomena' (BGE.108). Morality, in his view, is simply how values and meanings are perceived and organised in a particular time and place. A life shaped by the will to power embodies a morality of noble sentiment and mental strength, focused on the furtherance of creativity, personal growth, and self-overcoming. Master morality is thus an affirmation of oneself as the measure of all things:

> The noble type of man feels *himself* to be the determiner of values, he does not need to be approved of, he judges, 'what harms me is harmful in itself', he knows himself to be that which in general first accords honour to things, he *creates values*.
>
> (BGE.260; cf. GM.I.11)

Nietzsche likens the will to power to a muscle that flexes and strengthens through engagement with life's struggles. It enables one to 'stomach' life's challenges. For Nietzsche, being strong and powerful does not mean dominating or controlling life but mastering one's response to life's inevitable strife. The will to power allows us to create a sense of order and form out of the chaotic and conflicting impulses we experience, without deluding ourselves into thinking we are establishing fixed, absolute truths. 'To impose upon becoming the *character* of being—that is the supreme will to power' (KSA.12:7[54]: 312–13).

Architects and will to power

Nietzsche initially categorised architecture, alongside sculpture and epic poetry, as examples of Apollonian art in its purest form due to their rationalised, structured nature, which he saw as distinct, restrained, and immediately comprehensible (BT.1). In *The Birth of Tragedy* (1872), he contrasted this with Dionysian art, considering music as its purest expression, characterised by fluidity, non-figurative qualities, and unpredictability. However, by *Twilight of the Idols* (written in 1888 and published in 1889), Nietzsche revised his view, identifying architecture as a special aesthetic type tied to the will to power. While sculpture and epic poetry remained Apollonian visionary arts, music— after his fall-out with Wagner—became for Nietzsche, 'just the leftovers of a much fuller realm of emotional expression, a mere *residuum* of Dionysian histrionics', due to its 'immobilisation' of multiple senses, particularly, the 'muscular sense' (TI.X.10: 94). Unlike architecture, music fails to engage the body and evoke physiological responses. Nietzsche suggested that while different art forms have evolved into distinct types, typically aligning with either Apollonian or Dionysian tendencies, the craft of the *architect* represents neither a Dionysian nor an Apollonian state'. Architecture, in his later view, is no longer a pure Apollonian art form but rather an expression of the 'great act of will, the will that moves mountains, the intoxication of the great will that craves for art'. He elaborated as follows.

> The mightiest humans have always inspired the architect; the architect was always prone to the suggestion of power. An edifice is intended to display pride, victory over gravity, the will to power; architecture is a kind of power eloquence in forms that are now persuasive, even flattering, now simply imperative. The highest feeling of power and security is expressed in whatever has *grand style*. Power that no longer needs any excuse; that scorns giving pleasure; that answers gravely; that does not need to be corroborated; that exists without being conscious that it is being contradicted; that reposes within *itself*, fatalistically, a law among laws: *that* speaks of itself as grand style.
>
> (TI.X.11: 94–5)

In unpublished drafts of this passage,

Nietzsche characterised the architect as 'a great act of willing in its most convincing and proudest form', and described architecture as 'the edifice of power' and 'the eloquence of the will in spatial forms', where 'the will to power' is 'made visible' and the 'soul's loquacity' is 'writ large' (KSA.14[117]: 425).

Nietzsche clearly believed that modern German architecture did not express the will to power. Their designs, in his view, were mere assembly projects carried out by those who were weak of will. In contrast, architects who could design according to their will to power were able to create unified styles. These buildings required no justification for their designs, they did not aim to please, and did not depend on past successes by imitating other designs. They answered only to themselves. According to architectural historian Fritz Neumeyer, Nietzsche, in this passage, commits himself to valuing architecture as the most powerful art form. For Nietzsche, Neumeyer explains, architecture represents an unconditional obligation to this world, to an 'architecture of being', and this commitment to securing one's sense of self is the 'hallmark' of giving style to one's character (2001/2004: 183).

Importantly, Nietzsche did not intend for this positive architecture to be appreciated solely by the architect. While a design will reflect the architect's unified will, that will aligns with the existential needs of the cultures and societies for which the architect designs. The architect is attuned to these needs and seeks to address them through their work. Buildings created in this way express the architect's will to power, but they also empower others who interact with them. In this respect, the architect is a precursor to the Übermensch. Although Nietzsche did not explain the causal relations that underpin this architectural experience, we can infer from his definition of art that it involves physiological experiences of increased strength and vitality—traits he attributed to a powerful will. He suggested that an architect or artist in such a position will 'impart', 'force', and 'enrich' their designs until they, too, are 'swelled' and 'overloaded with strength' (TI.IX.8–9: 93). These designs will, in turn, express distinctive characteristics, embodying the will of the architect or artist in spatial form. Moreover, Nietzsche implied that individuals who exercise their will to power are better equipped to recognise this kind of architecture and more receptive to its transformative impact.

Thus, the architect who exercises their will to power organises the needs of their culture and society into a unified style, which they then render into 'eloquent' forms that inspire and uplift others (TI.IX.11: 94). Nietzsche seems to have had a similar experience when observing the Genoese palazzi, as discussed in Chapter 2. He admired these buildings because they reflected the fulfilled lives of their creators as spatial representations of their will to power.

Nietzsche described how each building captures the single-minded vision and mastery of its creator, showcasing a 'singular taste that sets itself apart from its neighbour as distinct and self-sufficient'. Although each palazzo has a different design, together they suggest to Nietzsche a unity of style, marked by their shared 'thirst for something new' (GS.291). The will to power is evident in the way the buildings assert themselves, expressing the creators' confidence in having '*lived*' and their desire 'to live on'. For Nietzsche, these buildings had a profound, evocative impact—they were not just objects to be observed from a distance, but rather constructions that invited him to engage with their design and to reflect on their influence. As he observed their designs, Nietzsche found himself drawn into a reverie, carried by his imagination into their construction. He envisaged the creators of these buildings pausing to admire their work, contemplating their diverse and accomplished lives, having built 'near and far', across 'city, sea, and mountain contours'. Nietzsche believed the powerful emotions and imagery of his, Nietzsche's, dream-like experience were 'incorporated' and infused into the fabric of the buildings themselves.

Efforts have been made to interpret Nietzsche's account of the transformative power of architecture and the effect of the architect's will to power on the observer of their designs. Nietzsche's suggestion that the formal qualities of architecture influence a person physiologically and psychologically foreshadows widely recognised theories in architectural history, such as Heinrich Wölfflin's seminal work, *Prolegomena to a Psychology of Architecture* (1886/2017), which proposed an empathetic relationship between architectural forms and bodily experience. Wölfflin's general premise echoes ideas Nietzsche had presented years earlier. For instance, while Nietzsche remarked that we are keen to 'translate ourselves into stone', that we 'stroll' within 'ourselves' as we would in a building (GS.280), and that our 'value and meaning' are determined from our nature as if '*a stone in a great edifice*' (GS.356), Wölfflin similarly compared the act of scrutinising a building to 'feeling every muscle in one's body' (Buddensieg 1999: 267). However, drawing attention to parallels like this does not mean that Wölfflin was influenced by Nietzsche. Both thinkers can be seen as part of a long tradition of finding correspondences between architectural forms and the human body—a tradition dating back to the Roman architect Vitruvius and continuing through more modern and contemporary theorists such as Maurice Merleau-Ponty (1908–61), and Juhani Pallasmaa in *The Eyes of the Skin* (1996).

Nietzsche suggested that buildings can speak and converse with people. I mentioned his reverie when observing the Genoese palazzi, but another notable instance occurred when he felt 'a soul' speaking from within the colossal stones of a Greek temple at Paestum, Italy (HHI.145). This experience may have been influenced by Jacob Burckhardt's commentary in *Der Cicerone*, where he describes the temples at Paestum as 'living beings' rather than inert or 'mere stone' (1855: 2). Nietzsche was particularly disparaging of ecclesiastical buildings, which 'speak much that is too emotional and too partisan' (GS.280), as well as modern German architecture, which he dismissed for its idle 'chatter' (GM.III.8).

Although buildings may mislead with their superficial chatter, a person who exercises their will to power can sift through the noise and find insights that inspire their own creative reflections.

One of the most detailed discussions of the relationship between architectural forms and the psycho-physiological experiences they evoke, within a Nietzschean context, is found in Paul Kühn's 1904 guidebook for the Nietzsche archive, which was intended as a philosophical critique of the renovations to Villa Silberblick, a building in Weimar that housed and continues to house Nietzsche's archives. The architect who undertook the renovations, at the request of Elisabeth Förster-Nietzsche, was Henry van de Velde. While I will explore van de Velde's designs that honour Nietzschean philosophy in the next chapter, here I want to focus on Kühn's analysis of van de Velde's renovations of Villa Silberblick, particularly his explanation of how architectural design can embody and evoke the will to power. Kühn's evaluation of van de Velde's ability to channel the will to power through his design closely mirrors the theory of ornament proposed by American modernist architect Louis H. Sullivan. Though Sullivan is best known for designing skyscrapers in American cities in the late nineteenth century, he was also notably influenced by Nietzschean philosophy, particularly *Thus Spoke Zarathustra*, of which Sullivan owned a well-worn copy.

Sullivan's account of the power of ornamental forms implicitly references the architect's will, which, he maintained, is aligned with the cultural needs of society. Given Sullivan's interest in Nietzschean philosophy, we can interpret his ideas on ornament—as Kühn did with van de Velde's use of patterned lines—as an application of Nietzsche's will to power in architectural design.

After discussing the accounts of Kühn and Sullivan, I will highlight several key aspects of the will to power as reflected in architectural designs more generally. These features include rhythmic patterns, minimalist ornamentation, and the drive to push at the boundaries of innovation. Together, these elements form what Nietzsche considered to be powerful architectural designs. Throughout my discussion, I will reference two architects who were arguably the most significant architects to influence Nietzsche—Gottfried Semper, whom Nietzsche called 'the most significant living architect', and Alessandro Antonelli, whose building in Turin, the Mole Antonelliana, Nietzsche praised as 'the greatest work of genius ever built' (GMD.18; KSA.1: 522; KSB.8.1227: 565, 656). Semper's theories offered Nietzsche valuable insights into the interplay of Dionysian and Apollonian forces in art, along with the importance of architectural surfaces enlivened by rhythmic, 'festive' elements. In contrast, Antonelli captivated Nietzsche with his relentless drive to challenge architectural limits by exercising his will to power.

Designing with will to power: Henry van de Velde and Louis H. Sullivan

Paul Kühn's account (1904) draws on van de Velde's theory of 'line-force' (1902) to explain how the Belgian architect fashioned his materials into a rhythmic composition that unifies and energises the instincts of the observer. For van de Velde, these patterned lines were not simply decorative, but a rhythmic force capable of animating the distinctive qualities of his design materials, thereby uplifting the spirits of those who encountered them. Much of Kühn's discussion focuses on the powerful impact of van de Velde's renovations of Villa Silberblick, emphasising the architect's use of abstract linear forms, his manipulation of light and shadow, and choice of materials. These elements, Kühn argued, provoke emotions in the viewer, culminating in a heightened experience akin to that which Nietzsche associates with enlightened, self-aware individuals.

With echoes of Nietzsche, Kühn noted that van de Velde's design does not distract visitors with superficial ornamentation; instead, its decoration is limited to what is 'necessary' to 'give strength and life' to the observer, instilling in them a 'life-awakening function' (1904: 23). At the same time, Kühn endorses van de Velde's rejection of historical styles and aligns the architect's vision of a future artistic age with Nietzsche's own (Kühn, 1904: 37). Kühn's criticisms of the replication of ornament continue to echo Nietzschean themes, condemning it as a 'disgusting masquerade', both of 'vain illusion' and a 'depraved imagination'. The 'parasitic' elements of a new building designed in historical styles, Kühn argued, 'disturb' its overall 'clarity and logic', establishing an unhealthy separation between people and their surroundings. Historicist architecture, he asserted, generates an 'immoral effect' that hinders the contemplation of 'honesty and unity' (Kühn, 1904: 34).

Kühn praised van de Velde's work as a much-needed Nietzschean remedy for cultural malaise. He believed Villa Silberblick enriched all who visited by functioning as a *Gesamtkunstwerk*, or 'total artwork', which integrated and elevated the spirit of its visitors and modern culture generally through van de Velde's 'new style'. According to Kühn, this new style generated rhythmic energy and meaningful, uplifting physical experiences, achieved through van de Velde's mastery of the line and his sensitivity to the organic qualities of his materials. It is as if, Kühn suggested, the materials themselves spoke to van de Velde, urging him to shape them in a way that highlighted their natural beauty, as though 'creative thoughts grow out of the material itself' (Kühn, 1904: 31). Van de Velde, in turn, 'awakens' these materials, ensuring that 'the spirit of heaviness leaves them', revealing their joyful nature (Kühn, 1904: 30, 31). Once you 'discover that the beauty of the wood is in its veining, and the delicacy of its inlay', Kühn argued, you will no longer desire 'to cover large, smooth surfaces with ornaments' (p. 30).

<u>When 'awakened material' is fashioned into forceful lines, the design is 'armed' with a powerful unity and rhythm that 'imparts strength and life', creating an 'absolute impression of unity' comparable to a 'symphony' (pp. 23, 26).</u>

This 'joyous' impression had a physiological effect on visitors to Villa Silberblick, encouraging a deeper integration of their sense of self. Echoing Nietzsche's definition of art as a 'frenzy of an overarched and swollen will' leading to feelings of 'increased strength and fullness' (TI.IX.8–9: 93), Kühn similarly described how van de Velde's design activates a 'latent force' that 'swells the limbs from the inside', encouraging visitors to 'feel a play of forces flowing through and directed by a central will' (Kühn, 1904: 26). As a result, those who enter the house are 'moved rhythmically' and their 'attitude to life is transformed, heightened, strengthened and refined' (p. 21).

Louis H. Sullivan expressed similar ideas in his approach to architectural ornament, which, he asserted, is rooted in fundamental human instincts, will, and creativity. At the core of his theory is a notion of self-mastery that parallels Nietzsche's idea of the will to power, particularly Nietzsche's demand for a singular taste to govern and shape every aspect of the creative work. In his essay, 'Ornament and Architecture' (1892), Sullivan explored the indivisible connection between the creation of ornament and the character and individuality of the architect. He suggested that if the architect can master their instincts, they will produce noble, harmonious designs that uplift and invigorate others. A powerful, effective building, according to Sullivan, is one that channels the architect's 'emotion' and 'spirit' through its ornamental features, allowing the design to 'flow harmoniously' throughout the building (1892/2014: 188). Ornament, in this context, appears to grow organically from the architectural surface, as if it is a natural feature of the building rather than something 'stuck on' (1892/2014: 189). The surface and ornamentation of a building thus express the same spirit, each enhancing the other's impact. Sullivan further asserted that while 'an excellent and beautiful building may be designed that shall bear no ornament whatever', a 'decorated structure, harmoniously conceived' and 'well considered, cannot be stripped of its system of ornament without destroying its individuality' (p. 188).

The integrity of the architect's imagination is crucial to achieving harmonious design, and this hinges on their will to power. According to Sullivan, architects must maintain 'a high and sustained emotional tension' to focus on the 'subtle rhythms' of a singular idea without distraction. A weak architect, in contrast, is indecisive—unable to commit to one idea, prone to imitation, and likely to produce derivative designs that fail to 'wholly satisfy'. Only an architect at the peak of their abilities, Sullivan argued, can 'impart to passive materials a subjective or spiritual human quality', by being 'open' in 'enlightened sympathy' to 'the voice of our times' (1892/2014: 187). The architect's capacity for concentration and discernment is essential here. Sullivan warned modern architects that 'everything is against you', because you are enveloped in a 'mist of tradition'. To dispel this mist, they must 'reduce all thoughts, all activities, to the simple test of honesty', ultimately achieving 'an organic singleness of idea' (1906/2014: 232, 188).

If an architect can dedicate this level of mental effort to their designs, they may adopt a completely new attitude to their work and life—similar to the revaluation of values advocated by Nietzsche. Sullivan sought to express the difficulties and the rewards of this new attitude: 'You will be surprised to see how matters that you once deemed solid, fall apart; and, how things that you once deemed inconsequential take on a new and momentous significance. But in time your mind will clarify and strengthen', enabling you to develop the 'intellectual power' to distinguish between those things that promote the 'health' and the 'illness of a people' (1906/2014). Sullivan further asserted— echoing Nietzsche's notion of architecture as the 'eloquence of the will' and 'will to power' in 'spatial form' (KSA.14[117]: 425)—that the most effective buildings are those 'designed with sufficient depth of feeling and simplicity of mind; the more intense the heat' in which they were 'conceived, the more serene and noble' they will 'remain forever' as monuments of human 'eloquence' (Sullivan, 1892/2014: 188). Given the parallels between Nietzsche's idea of the will to power and the connection Sullivan made between the architect's mentality and the spirit of ornament, it is not surprising that Sullivan's concept of ornament has been described in terms resonant with the will to power and the figure of the Übermensch. As one scholar notes, Sullivan's ornament is an 'architecture of *striving*' (Van Zanten, 2000: 119).

The dance of design

In the examples above, the architect's will to power is infused in their designs, transferring to those who interact with them. This transfer occurs through the rhythmic interplay of forms, patterns, and textures, which are experienced by individuals as corresponding sensations and forces within their own bodies. When these sensations are aligned and directed by the individual's will to power, they can evoke feelings of uplift and rejuvenation, positively influencing their overall mindset and approach to life. The body and mind become invigorated as they engage with the powerful rhythms of the design. It is as if the visitor is invited to dance with the architecture. Van de Velde, in his essay, 'The Line', discusses how geometric lines create a 'powerful rhythm' that draws us in, moving us 'with the voluptuousness of a dancer' (1902: 160). Similarly, Kühn remarks that visitors to Villa Silberblick are 'animated by Zarathustra's dance rhythms' (1904: 14).

Dancing is an important motif in Nietzsche's work, frequently symbolising the presence of an invigorating spirit. Zarathustra declares, 'We should consider every day lost in which we have not danced at least once' (Z.III,12: 23). In his critique of the so-called 'higher men' of society, Zarathustra laments, 'The worst about you is none of you has learned to dance as a man ought to dance—to dance beyond yourselves!' (Z.IV.13: 3). Nietzsche also emphasised that no kind of '*dancing*' should be 'excluded from *noble education*', whether it be dancing with the 'feet, with concepts, or with words [...]' (TI.8.7: 87).

From a Nietzschean perspective, well-designed architecture invites bodily movement, evoking what he calls a '*grand* rhythm' and the 'rise and fall' of superhuman passion' (EH.II.4). However, this does not necessarily mean it must inspire an excitable or frenzied dance, of the kind associated with Dionysian revelries. Architecture can be equally uplifting and powerful through the subtle interplay of forms and textures. As I mentioned in Chapter 2, Nietzsche praised Luca Fancelli, the architect of the Palazzo Pitti, for designing in accordance with a raw will to power, reflected in the building's clear and straightforward style (KSA.3.226: 511). The simplicity of this large Renaissance palace evokes the rhythmic qualities of a structure shaped by the will to power (Figure 2). Its front elevation features a repetition of arched apertures across three floors, reminiscent of a Roman aqueduct. Each floor is edged with a simple stone railing, while large pietraforte sandstone blocks, quarried on-site, are rusticated with deep recesses between joints, giving the building a bold, solid appearance. Originally, the palace had three floors of equal length, resulting in a square façade. However, in the seventeenth century, the two lower floors were extended beyond the uppermost floor, creating two large wings. The uppermost floor originally had 7 arches, later extended to 13, while the floor below features 23. The lowest floor initially had just three large portals, expanded to include eight more windows with triangular pediments. With fewer apertures on the ground floor, more of the rusticated stone is exposed, enhancing the impression of a solid, impenetrable base. The contrast between the vast top floor, sitting on top of the extended floors below, was noted by Burckhardt as the building's

Figure 2 Palazzo Pitti, Florence (built 1458, Luca Fancelli). Front elevation. Postcard c.1910.

'special' feature, contributing to its powerful effect. Nietzsche, influenced by Burckhardt's assessment, was particularly struck by the Palazzo's clear style and rhythmic formal arrangement, which, for him, conveyed 'most intensely' the 'art of melody' (KSB.7.688: 177; KSA.9.197: 520; KSA.3.226: 511).

Nietzsche was critical of buildings that are too vast, 'bloated', and 'gigantic', with an 'inflated style' (D.161, 332). The imposing Palazzo Pitti could be seen as an example of this. The expansive surfaces of monumental structures can often surpass our bodily proportions, vanishing into the horizon, making them difficult to relate to. However, the Palazzo Pitti engaged with Nietzsche. Despite its monumental scale, its contours can be traced against the sky, maintaining Nietzsche's own presence rather than diminishing it. Its vastness is balanced by its melodic style. In the Palazzo Pitti, we encounter the Apollonian immediacy of its austere, rusticated solidity, enlivened by a Dionysian rhythmic play of its simple patterns.

The melodic rhythms of the Palazzo Pitti may seem subtle, yet they resonated with Nietzsche all the same. These rhythms are no less uplifting than the bold and expressive movements often associated with the Bauhaus school of design, architecture, and applied arts—particularly the geometric dance forms developed by Oskar Schlemmer. Schlemmer, a devoted reader of Nietzsche and one of Walter Gropius's earliest appointments to the Bauhaus, was given the title 'Master of Form'. His role involved exploring the relationship between geometric forms and their movement in space. In his diaries, Schlemmer credited Nietzsche's insights into the interplay of Apollonian and Dionysian forms as a key to shaping his own ideas. Schlemmer referred to Nietzsche as 'the philosopher of my youth' (1990: 24), and Nietzsche's influence remained central to Schlemmer's work throughout his life.

Schlemmer is perhaps best known for his experimental investigations into relationships between geometric forms and dance, through his creation of the *Triadic Ballet*, which he choreographed for the theatrical stage at the Bauhaus school. In this ballet, dancers wore colourful, minimalist costumes, each representing one of three fundamental shapes: triangle, square, and circle. The costumes intentionally restricted movement, resulting in robotic, mechanical gestures that were designed to express geometric pathways of colour and shape moving through space. Schlemmer envisioned this abstract ballet as a response to German expressive dance, positioning it as a reinvention of an abstract art form. He dismissed German expressive dance as chaotic and Dionysian, while celebrating his *Triadic Ballet* in explicitly Apollonian terms (Schlemmer 1990: 69). However, if Schlemmer sought to supress Dionysian aesthetics in favour of abstract Apollonian art, as he himself suggested, he exemplifies the very modern tendencies that Nietzsche criticised and aimed to overcome.

Ornament: non-distracting, surface rhythms

If an architect designs from a position of will to power, with a coordinated and unified style, they will reject frivolous aesthetics and abandon outdated blueprints and models to focus on bold, simple, and distinctive designs born from their own imagination, risks, and experiments. This does not imply that Nietzsche advocated for buildings devoid of ornamentation or decoration.

His call to focus on what is essential, avoiding arbitrary 'chatter' and abstract contemplation, is not a plea for an ascetic, featureless architecture of white-washed, blank walls.

A Nietzschean approach to architecture would engage the viewer instinctively and physiologically, and featureless designs might be as ineffective in this regard as the Christian buildings he berates for their fussy, symbolic ornamentation that promote 'intercourse with another world', offering a language that is too emotive and constrained 'for us godless people to think *our thoughts*' through them (GS.280). Instead, overly eclectic and busy decoration is more likely to distract, drawing attention to itself rather than encouraging a person to engage with their own immediate, bodily responses, compared to a simpler design, stripped to its 'necessary' features.

Once stripped of ornament and purged of idle chatter, architecture does not lose its ability to communicate; rather, it simply changes the way it expresses itself. It no longer 'talks' at a person but instead leverages the will to power to 'command' a more meaningful engagement, encouraging reflection not on the architecture itself but on the person themselves (cf. TI.IX.8: 92; GS.291). Nietzsche alluded to 'empty forms', which, in architectural terms, could signify the raw components of a structure—forms that are intentionally 'empty' to invite subjective, free interaction, allowing people to 'fill' them with personal thoughts and reflections. For Nietzsche, architecture built with empty forms represented a new kind of design, one that revives a more visceral connection to the material environment and revitalises personal creativity, free from distracting symbols that speak of times past and misleading ideologies.

According to art historian Tilmann Buddensieg, Nietzsche's perspective on empty form evolved from the period of *Human, All Too Human* in 1878, where it reflects a painful loss, to the occasions of his later visits to Genoa and Turin, where he celebrated its liberating nature (Buddensieg, 1999: 263). *Human, All Too Human* is often regarded as the beginning of Nietzsche's 'middle period' (including the book, *Daybreak* (1881) and the first four sections of *The Gay Science* (1882)), during which Nietzsche adopted a more moderate approach, aimed at exposing errors in judgement and questioning assumptions rather than advancing his own ideas. In this phase, he distanced himself from German Romanticism and Wagner, through the adoption of a more positivist stance that values science and reason.

In a cryptic aphorism from *Human, All Too Human*, titled *Stone is more stony than before* (HHI.218), Nietzsche criticised modern culture for habitually failing to appreciate the 'inexhaustible significance' and enchanting beauty of buildings. This lack of appreciation meant that buildings once capable of evoking profound responses—such as ancient 'Greek or Christian buildings' still standing today—were now devalued in the eyes of modern observers, who perceived them merely as stone assemblages devoid of deeper meaning. With this shift, architecture lost its power to move people, rendering buildings as mere 'empty' forms, nothing more than the materials from which they were made.

However, Nietzsche appeared to revise his stance on empty forms around 1880, following his visits to Genoa and Turin, where he finds himself captivated by secular architecture, palazzi, and arcaded streets. The loss of symbolic ornamentation, once seen as painful, now becomes a cultural gain; empty form takes on the potential for personal and cultural liberation, becoming a source of creative self-discovery. While Nietzsche initially mourned the inability to decipher buildings replete with symbolic signs, in a later aphorism from *The Gay Science* titled, *Architecture for the knower* (GS.280), he berates the emotive language of such buildings, which attempt still to speak, seduce, and engage observers with other-worldly ideals and outmoded values. Nietzsche's preference for empty forms contrasts starkly with the architectural examples I discussed in the previous chapter, which, as noted, represented for him the problematic tendencies of modern culture to distract, mislead, and supress creativity.

Although we might expect Nietzsche to have advocated the demolition of buildings that embody harmful ideals or point to other worlds, he was inclined to let them stand to allow them to be reinterpreted and repurposed. In this respect, he envisioned a sustainable architecture, where buildings can be adapted and reused as and when the needs of their users evolve. Derelict or obsolete buildings can regain significance, but only if they are stripped of their rhetorical elements and made *empty*. For Nietzsche, churches, temples, palaces, streets, marketplaces—indeed *any* built structures, when silenced—become spaces for self-reflection and architecture 'for those who *know* themselves'.

To me, a building's 'stony' quality suggests the nature of its raw materials. In this sense, a historic building that appears *more stony than before* signals the broken connection between its original architectural style and its present-day observers. The building no longer elicits much of a response in people today, who instead regard it at a distance, as a mere material object. Yet, Nietzsche later reconsidered this 'stony' quality, finding value in it. In this view, a building perceived purely through its raw, material presence appears 'more stony'—not as a sign of passivity or indifference, but as a means to rekindle a more meaningful connection between people and buildings. Architectural theorist Markus Breitschmid, reflecting on Nietzsche's notion of 'stony' quality, astutely remarks

> with the shift of the architectural essence of meaning [from the interior mind of intellectual contemplation] to the outside, it is the building's proportions, the outline, the straight and right-angled lines and edges, the surface, the unity of the body, which are decisive.
>
> (2001: 93)

Breitschmid's description of architectural 'essence' highlights the fundamental, *necessary* elements of design. Drawing from Kühn's interpretation of van de Velde's commanding designs, we could further enrich this description with the organic qualities of the materials themselves.

Festive surfaces: Gottfried Semper

While van de Velde regarded simple linear ornament as the most fundamental, rhythmic element that animated and enlivened architectural surfaces, Semper viewed geometric ornament as the true festive origin of architecture. Like Nietzsche, Semper sought to revive the passions and excitement inspired by ancient Greek culture within German culture. While eighteenth- and nineteenth-century portrayals often cast the Greeks as rational people, striving for virtue through Apollonian ideals of clarity and uniformity—reflected in their architecture through symmetrical and harmonious proportions—Nietzsche and Semper (and Wagner, who had befriended them both) were drawn to the more dramatic and irrational experiences celebrated by the ancient Greeks.

Semper's interest began with the debate over whether Greek monuments were originally white or coloured. Semper argued for their polychromy and his empirical investigations into the original hues of ancient buildings led him to consider the social significance of coloured surfaces and coverings more generally, which led to the conclusion that architecture's roots coincided with the origins of textiles. He proposed that the first enclosures were woven materials, which evolved into more sophisticated forms with coloured patterns. For Semper, the surface cladding of a building—its colourful covering—expressed cultural values more vividly than the building's overall structure (1860/2004: 248–50). This view contrasted with conventional theories about the origins of architecture, especially the common belief that the primitive hut was the original architectural form. Instead, Semper argued that the origins of architecture were in 'festive celebration', with the earliest architectural structures resembling a ceremonial stage, 'hung with tapestries, dressed with festoons and garlands, and decorated with fluttering banners and trophies'. Such adornment, he claimed, motivated the creation of lasting monuments, intended to commemorate celebratory acts or events for future generations (p. 249).

For Semper, all buildings, regardless of their function, trace their origins back to the colours and textures of the theatrical stage. One might question whether Semper's emphasis on surface cladding and colourful adornment conflicts with Nietzsche's desire for stripping architectural surfaces of unnecessary distractions. However, Semper's focus is on the *spirit* of festivity conveyed by these adornments, not on the adornments themselves. What matters is the surface's dynamic quality and its ability to evoke a 'festive' atmosphere—an interest shared by both Semper and Nietzsche.

For Semper, as for Nietzsche, architecture is meant to be an experience to participate in, rather than a mere object to observe.

Nietzsche believed that architecture, when stripped of distracting decor, allows the observer to engage more fully in its celebratory spirit.

> Oh, those Greeks! [Nietzsche exclaims] They knew how to *live*: what is needed for that is to stop bravely at the surface, the fold, the skin; to adore appearance, to believe in shapes, tones, words—in the whole Olympus of appearance! Those Greeks were superficial—*out of profundity!*
>
> (GS.Preface.4)

The empty surfaces Nietzsche sought are far from sterile; they animate and engage the onlooker on a profound level.

In Chapter 3, I highlighted the shared concerns of Nietzsche and Semper regarding the inclination of modern German architecture to replicate past styles, exposing a lack of original thought and failure to capture a more festive spirit. Semper identifies several issues that contributed to this situation, including the increasing fragmentation of the arts into separate specialisations during the nineteenth century, which weakened their cohesion and impact. Additionally, the rise of industrial production toward the end of the century outpaced artistic mastery, resulting in products and designs of inferior quality. To illustrate the problematic direction of architecture, Semper critiqued the approach of French architect Jean-Nicholas Louis Durand (1760–1834), whose teachings stressed symmetry and uniformity, as seen in his designs for German towns like Mannheim and Karlsruhe. Durand's method involved drawing square grids onto which building plans were routinely plotted and arranged. This simple system was taught to engineering students from 1795 at the newly established École Polytechnique in Paris, with the astonishing claim that any first-year student could become a fully trained architect after just six months of training in this method. Semper found this claim absurd. He mocked it, suggesting it could enable architects to perform architectural 'miracles' across entire cities. According to Semper, a graduate of Durand's school 'loses himself' in the 'lifeless schematism' of this method, which merely 'combines' and 'lines up things superficially', creating a 'mechanical' unity rather than an 'organic working together around the primary, animating idea' (Semper 1852/2010: 169). Nietzsche would have argued that this rigid approach is missing a compensatory Dionysian impulse to allow the design to break free of strict visual constraints, and to infuse a sense of lyricism and playfulness into otherwise characterless designs and instil confidence in students to exercise their will to power. This would allow students the opportunity to channel their imaginative vision, leading to more unified and more creative architectural designs.

There are several points of convergence between Semper's architectural theories and Nietzsche's remarks on architecture, which together help explain why Nietzsche lauds Semper as 'the most significant living architect'. However, it is probably Semper's emphasis on non-rational artistic impulses that gives Nietzsche's praise most weight, as Semper's ideas seem to have shaped Nietzsche's understanding of both the interplay of Dionysian and Apollonian forces in art, and the need to elevate the Dionysian to revive a culture that is overly fixated on Apollonian ideals. While Nietzsche's early discussion of these contrasting forces is most fully developed in *The Birth of Tragedy* (1872), its origins can be traced to earlier public lectures he wrote in 1870 and his preparatory notes for these, which reference several of Semper's works, including *Style in the Technical and Tectonic Arts* (1860/2004), his essay 'Preliminary Remarks of Polychrome Architecture and Sculpture in Antiquity' (1834/2010), and his lecture 'On Architectural Styles' (1869/2010).

Architectural theorist Fritz Neumeyer has demonstrated that Nietzsche appears to have structured his 1870 lecture, 'The Greek Music Drama', to reflect the same sequence of arguments that Semper employs in his essay on polychromy, with Nietzsche simply substituting Semper's architectural references with examples from drama. When read side by side, the two texts show a striking parallel (Neumeyer 2001/2004: 37). In his lecture, Nietzsche argued that the surviving tragic plays of ancient Greece are poor copies of richer choral works that preceded them, and he challenged the prevalent belief of his time that music was a secondary element in ancient tragedies, subordinate to plot and dialogue. This mistaken belief, he contended, distorts the true nature and significance of tragedy, much like those who dismissed the idea that ancient sculpture was originally adorned in vibrant colours (GMD.8). Just as Semper argued that vivacious claddings of ancient Greek architecture expressed the vitality of ancient Greek values, Nietzsche maintained that the musical power of ancient tragedies conveyed an equally essential and overlooked vitality.

Nietzsche went on to explore ancient choral song, attributing its potency to the evocation of Dionysian frenzy, which encouraged the audience to merge with the tragic performance. In his preparatory notes, Nietzsche illustrated his point with a phrase taken from Semper's *Style in the Technical and Tectonic Arts* (1860/2004), writing: 'The haze of carnival candles is the true atmosphere of art, Semper, p. 231' (KSA,7.1[21]: 16). In Semper's public lecture, 'On Architectural Styles' (1869)—a text Nietzsche read and gifted to Richard and Cosima Wagner—Semper speaks of the need to reconcile 'two seemingly contradictory cultural forces: namely, striving towards individuality and merging into the collective' (1869/2010: 281). These two forces closely align with Nietzsche's own concepts of Apollo and Dionysus.

Beyond boundaries: designing for new heights and expanding horizons

Animation is essential to good architectural design, and a feeling of empowerment is just as vital. Nietzsche described this empowerment as a physical sensation, an experience of 'increased strength and fullness', and 'easy, bold, exuberant, self-assured rhythms' (TI.IX.8–9: 92–3; GS.368). This connection between architecture and body aligns with Semper's idea of festivity at the architectural surface, and perhaps even more vividly in van de Velde's portrayal of linear ornament, which moves us 'with the voluptuousness of a dancer, balancing, turning her body, throwing her arms and legs in the air' (2003: 160). The architect's will to power becomes visible and tangible through the buildings' structural forces and ornamental features. This effect is evident in the compression, tension, and upward thrust of Sullivan's skyscrapers, which draw the observer into their visceral architectural drama, activating muscular sensations in their body. Architectural historian Vincent Scully identifies this effect in Sullivan's Guaranty building in Buffalo, New York (built in 1894–5 and renamed the Prudential building in 1898). Its design employs subtle ornamentation to transform the simple skeleton of slender steel members into a structure clad 'with what appears to be integral force, stepping out towards its corner, standing, stretching, and physically potent' (Scully 1959: 75). Scully adds, 'One can feel in Sullivan's buildings, a curious power of potential action'. He imagines that if one were to turn one's back to the Guaranty building, it might take a 'giant step across the square' (p. 80).

The Palazzo Pitti encourages an immediate physical response of 'strength and fullness' through the unyielding solidity of its expansive stone mass and 'self-assured rhythms' in the repetition of its simple forms and textures. Later in his writings, Nietzsche became increasingly captivated by experiences and analogies of elevation. By emphasising height rather than mass, Nietzsche highlighted the contrast between his affirmative philosophy and the decadent cultural values he perceived in modern Germany, which he had associated with heaviness, density, and the 'spirit of gravity' or the 'great weight'. What better way, then, to express the triumph over heaviness and gravity than a powerful upward movement of mass?

In *Twilight of the Idols* (1889/2021), Nietzsche observed that 'an edifice is intended to display pride, victory over gravity, the will to power' (TI.X.11: 94–5). Throughout his writings, he contrasted mediocre architecture—characterised by monotonous, standardised forms along a horizontal plane—with noble architecture, which embodies varied and towering forms. Nietzsche criticised 'peasant houses' with their 'low and depressed' rooms, finding them uninhabitable as they 'always cause restlessness' (KSB.6.427: 387). This contrasts with the pleasure he found in elevated apartments with high ceilings and expansive views to the horizon, spaces that, as noted in Chapter 2, he felt were 'good for my mood' and 'beneficial for my sleep'.

Nietzsche conceptualises cultural malaise and its remedy, the exercise of will to power, in spatial terms, where will to power is a dynamic force driving upwards to elevated positions. Cultural malaise lacks this upward movement; it is inert, stagnant, and weighed down, devoid of power or inclined to supress positive power in favour of democratic values that flatten individual enterprise.

By exercising the will to power, individuals can rise above the status quo, distancing themselves from limiting influences and gaining a broader vision of the horizon ahead, which encourages innovation and creative vision beyond the constraints of ground-level perspectives.

Nietzsche saw modern German architecture as in desperate need of this 'uplift'. 'Suppose I were to step out of my house', he wrote, and find a 'small German town: my instinct would have to put up barricades to repel anything assaulting it from this flat and cowardly world' (EH.II.8: 242). From Nietzsche's perspective, most German towns were stunted and flattened by the weight of oppressive values that their inhabitants upheld. Buddensieg suggests that Nietzsche was probably referring to the 'intricately timber-framed cities of modern, medieval domestic architecture—Halle, Naumburg, Cologne, Basel, and Strasbourg—those he himself had seen as "cowering" beneath the sway of vast cathedrals' (1999: 263)

To affirm life and achieve self-mastery, one must aspire to reach the heights.

<u>Life [Nietzsche declared] wants to build itself high with columns and stairs; it wants to gaze into the far distance and out upon joyful splendour—*that* is why it needs height! And because it needs height, it needs steps […]. Life wants to climb and in climbing overcome itself […] (Z.II.29: 125)</u>

The Genoese palazzi embody this height instinct, standing as bold, self-assured buildings that reflect the vitality of their creators—those who, as Nietzsche observes, *celebrated life through* their buildings. However, it was the Mole Antonelliana towering over Turin that captured this height instinct most viscerally for Nietzsche, embodying the architecture of life that Zarathustra described (Figure 3). Built *high with columns and stairs*, the Mole *gazes into the far distance*, aligning seamlessly with Nietzsche's vision. *Thus Spoke Zarathustra* continues as if describing the Mole and its architect, Alessandro Antonelli:

'Here he who once towered aloft his thoughts in stone, knew as well as the wisest about the secret of life! [...] How divinely vault and arch here contrast one another in the struggle: how they strive against one another with light and shadow, these divinely-striving things' (Z.II.29:125).

The Mole Antonelliana appears to transform Nietzsche's metaphor into a concrete reality. Nietzsche regarded it as 'the greatest work of genius ever built out of an absolute instinct for height—suggestive of nothing so much as my *Zarathustra*. I have christened it "Ecce Homo" and mentally surrounded it with an immense open space' (Letter to Köselitz, KSB.8.1227: 565, 656). *Ecce Homo* ('Behold the Man') (1908/2021) was the title of Nietzsche's final work, a quasi-autobiography in which he interprets his own significance, development, and writings. Naming the Mole after this book suggests the deep connection Nietzsche felt with the building. In a postscript to his letter to Köselitz, he even highlighted the parallel between his book and the architect, noting that Antonelli 'lived just as long, until *Ecce Homo*, the book was finished—The book and the human being' (KSB.8.1227: 656). Antonelli died on 18 October 1888, and Nietzsche completed his book less than three weeks later, though he continued to revise it until 6 January 1889 (and it would not be published until 1908, after Nietzsche's death).

This was not the first time Nietzsche linked the completion of a work to the death of a significant figure. In *Ecce Homo*, he mentions that 'the closing section' of *Thus Spoke Zarathustra* 'was completed precisely at that sacred hour when Richard Wagner died in Venice' (EH.IX.Z.1). As architectural theorist Jörg H. Gleiter points out, 'Twice, one of his books became the legacy of an artist: *Zarathustra* and the composer, *Ecce Homo* and the architect' (2009: 48, cf.20). Nietzsche once revered both artists, yet it seems the legacy of Antonelli, through the Mole, offered Nietzsche a counterbalance to the decadent influence he saw in Wagner. While the Palazzo Pitti had expressed to him a vivid melody and bold, merry tempo (KSB.7.688: 177), the Mole Antonelliana, with its powerful rhythms, embodied the architectural experience he sought—a place where he could metaphorically walk within himself, discovering a renewed sense of self.

Figure 3 Mole Antonelliana, Turin (built 1863–89, Alessandro Antonelli). Front elevation. Author's photograph.

In the Mole Antonelliana, Nietzsche found a powerful architectural embodiment of the will to power—the drive to build ever higher, achieve greater feats, and pursue ambitious innovation. For Nietzsche, the Mole reaches its towering height not simply because it is physically tall but because it manifests the relentless will to power of its architect. Despite financial setbacks and the withdrawal of his benefactors, Antonelli stubbornly refused to compromise on his design, determined to push beyond the dictates of architectural conventions even at considerable risk. Disregarding the approved plans and administrative consent to build to a height of 47 metres, Antonelli drastically modified the design, ultimately raising it to an imposing 167.5 metres. These radical changes threatened to scupper the entire project. According to the official guidebook to the Mole Antonelliana, Antonelli was spurred on by 'a never-ending "need" to surpass every limit' imposed by either 'authorities or nature'. It further notes that this insatiable drive to achieve his vision, coupled with his disregard for client expectations, made him 'an obstinate experimenter, a severe, strict innovator, prepared to risk isolation, incomprehension, and criticism' (Cimorelli, 2016: 5–6). Antonelli's approach reflects a Nietzschean will to power. As Fritz Neumeyer observes, Nietzsche deeply identified with a building that exemplified the human potential to create through sheer force of will (2001/2004: 248).

The Mole's lightweight, wide-spanned, vaulted masonry structure was remarkably innovative for its time. Construction historian David Wendlend regards it as 'one of the outstanding masterpieces in the history of architecture' due to 'its structural and architectural concepts' (2007: 2). Wendlend describes Antonelli's construction system as 'revolutionary' for its skeleton of slender piers, horizontal flat arches, and lightweight, flat vaults. Antonelli effectively adapted innovations from iron construction to masonry, and his systematic use of iron rods in the Mole, Wendlend argues, can be considered 'the invention of reinforced masonry' (2007). Civil engineers Chiara Calderini and Luisa Pagnini also highlight the building's pioneering construction, observing that Antonelli's extensive use of metallic ties 'is impressive' and renders the structure nearly comparable 'to modern frame buildings' (Calderini and Pagnini, 2015).

The dome of the Mole towers above Turin and is visible from almost any part of the city, which is a reason why it is considered by locals as a symbol of the city. The building has a robust, square base in a Neo-classical style, featuring large pilasters and arches that frame the entrance. Inside, there are several levels (not conventional storeys) as well as a large hall. Above the hall, the building tapers into an octagonal drum and then transitions to an elongated dome. The dome is constructed with a double shell, each only 12 cm thick, and its transition from a square to an octagonal base with a rounded dome exemplifies Antonelli's experimental approach of merging contrasting geometric forms to create a dynamic structure. The dome's surface is minimally adorned with cornices, mouldings, reliefs, semicircular windows and openings that illuminate the interior. Above the dome is a cupola that holds a viewing platform offering panoramic views of Turin and the Alps. Since 1961, this platform has been accessible via a glass lift, giving views of the interior as it ascends. The platform then extends through several layers into a long, slender spire crowned by a pinnacle.

According to Gleiter, the defining quality of the Mole Antonelliana is not its height or innovative engineering but its eclectic style, expressed through 'the linearity and arrangement of its different architectural elements' (2009: 58). This eclecticism is most apparent in the pinnacle, where various geometric forms are stacked in succession. At the base sits a two-level square lantern with pediments, followed by a truncated cone that transitions the square section into a circular shape. Above this is a cylindrical section, which divides first into a double ring of supports, then into a second ring, and finally culminates in an octagonal pyramid. Originally, a star topped the pinnacle, later replaced by a 'winged genius' statue between 1889 and 1904, until a storm dislodged it and a star was restored.

When Nietzsche identified with the Mole, its exterior was nearing completion, undergoing consolidation of the spire and drum following an earthquake on 23 February 1887. The Mole's ability to withstand severe weather could be seen symbolically as an existential test of its vitality, its power to remain 'noble', 'upright', and true to itself despite continuous challenges. As noted in the official guidebook, the building's resilience following damage caused to its pinnacle—the most fragile and least anchored part—showcases it as having 'a vitality of its own, able to adapt to environmental changes' that ultimately 'proved pessimists wrong' (Cimorelli, 2016: 12). Nietzsche was probably aware of the building's resilience in this respect. By withstanding the impact of unforeseen forces and defying the sceptics—or 'nay-sayers', as Nietzsche might describe them—the Mole Antonelliana is a veritable embodiment of the will to power and the vital 'yea-saying instinct' (Z.III.IV: 184–7; GS.276).

Despite such praise, the Mole is seldom highlighted in literature in the history of architecture, and is sometimes dismissed altogether, with art historian Tilman Buddensieg noting it is often ridiculed as a 'monster' for its eclectic design (1999: 266). However, it was generally lauded by contemporaries of Nietzsche and Antonelli; some described it as a 'formidable stairway to the sky' (Guillén, 2006: 69). Its deviation from established architectural styles and its lack of a distinctive name or purpose suggest an 'empty form', which may have attracted Nietzsche to it as an architectural structure that fostered introspection, self-reflection, and ultimately a celebration of its capacity to bring him closer to himself.

German architecture for the German spirit?

The buildings I have described as favoured by Nietzsche are primarily from Northern Italy, and this is telling when it comes to considering the question of how 'German' a new architecture would have to be in Nietzsche's summation if it were to revive the spirit of modern German culture. Nietzsche believed that we should draw lessons from history and past cultures on what could be nourishing for our own. He saw ancient Greek culture as a model for the creative renewal he envisioned for Germany—not through imitation of Greek art forms or classical architecture, but by understanding how the Greeks captured the spirit of their time, balancing Apollonian and Dionysian forces in their art. Nietzsche's willingness to look outside Germanic myths and traditions for cultural renewal suggests that a modern architectural design shaped organically by this spirit would not be limited to Germanic architectural traditions.

The architectural styles established throughout Germany's history did not, in Nietzsche's view, capture the creative energy required to revitalise contemporary German architecture. In fact, he cautioned against creating solely within the narrow confines of national identity. Instead, he advocated that Germany should cast its gaze further afield to 'digest' and 'absorb' creative influences from other cultures (BGE.251; HHI.475). However, as Germany entered the twentieth century, it was marked by volatility and a pressure to consolidate a distinct national identity amidst rapid changes, which made the advantages of a broader, more cosmopolitan perspective less likely to be recognised.

CHAPTER 5

Nietzsche's architects

In this final chapter, I examine various architectural designs and approaches that were intended to honour or represent Nietzschean ideas. It is interesting to see how they fare in light of Nietzsche's own assessments of poor and powerful architecture. My survey begins with a building that could be considered the first architectural structure to be linked with, and possibly inspired by Nietzsche's ideas. While the evidence to suggest a direct association with Nietzsche and Nietzschean ideas is tenuous and contentious, it is nevertheless an interesting building to consider in the context of Nietzsche's understanding of the relationship between Dionysus and Apollo and his desire to revive modern European culture by promoting Dionysian forces. The building is the Semperoper, designed in 1879 by Gottfried Semper, who, as I have noted, was lauded by Nietzsche as 'the most significant living architect' of his time. The Semperoper was Semper's second opera house in Dresden, built to replace his first after it was destroyed by fire.

Aside from Gottfried Semper and Alessandro Antonelli, Nietzsche regarded the architects of his day as lacking the creative genius to harness their will to power and to engage with the spirit of the time. He subsequently described contemporary artists as 'unsuitable building material' (GS.356). Nevertheless, architects maintained a superior position in Nietzsche's vision for spiritual and cultural renewal. Although they are not Übermenschen, they have the potential to become artistic leaders and visionaries. With this potential comes a great responsibility to address the needs of their communities through thoughtful and impactful designs. In the late nineteenth and twentieth centuries, many architects, including Le Corbusier and Louis H. Sullivan, sought to present themselves as heroic artists or prophets of a new culture and design style, even modelling themselves after Nietzsche's prophet, Zarathustra.

Secular temple buildings

Designing and constructing a distinctly 'Nietzschean' building presents obvious challenges. Even if there were some consensus on the meaning of Nietzsche's philosophical vision—a problematic task in itself—translating his ideas into three-dimensional, spatial forms would be extremely difficult. Despite these obstacles, several architects have endeavoured to create buildings that embody Nietzsche's philosophy. The secular temple is the most prevalent building type among these examples. In the nineteenth century such structures represented a desire for a different and more fulfilling life, reflecting the ideals of either the client who commissioned it or the individual commemorated by it. Though intended to be secular, these temples often acquired a sacred aura, as admirers revered the ideals embodied in their designs.

In Chapter 3 I mentioned a passage from *Genealogy of Morals* where Nietzsche spoke of the need for quiet, hidden places where one can escape the distracting 'noise' of 'democratic chatter' and the 'junk' of modern life (GM. III.8). In this passage, Nietzsche referred to the courtyards and colonnades of the Temple of Artemis, where the philosopher Heraclitus retreated from the distractions of his time. Nietzsche initially laments the lack of similar temple spaces in contemporary cities, but his tone shifts when he nostalgically recalls his 'beautiful study, the Piazzo di San Marco' in Venice during the springtime, between the hours of ten and noon. This memory seems to soften his stance on the absence of temple-like spaces in his day, leading him to acknowledge that such spaces 'are *not* lacking' after all. In fact, he generously concedes that 'even a room in a busy, ordinary guest house', where one can remain anonymous and talk freely, can sometimes suffice.

<u>While Nietzsche advocated temple-like buildings as places for reflection and may have recognised their presence in the vernacular architecture of his time, he is firmly opposed to temples</u>

designed for worship or any structure meant to idolise his ideas or those of others.

In *Ecce Homo*, Nietzsche states, 'I *want* no "believers". I think I am too malicious to believe in myself; I never speak to masses—I have a terrible fear that one day I will be pronounced *holy*' (EH.XIV). Through his prophetic figure, Zarathustra, Nietzsche desires not disciples or followers, but listeners and seekers. To his unwanted acolytes, he issues a stern architectural warning: 'Take care, lest a falling a statue [or, perhaps, a building] strike you dead!' (Z.I.22[3]: 103).

The buildings discussed in this chapter include several key projects. Among them are Henry van de Velde's renovations of Villa Silberblick in Weimar (1902–3), commissioned by Nietzsche's sister, Elisabeth Förster-Nietzsche, to preserve Nietzsche's legacy and house his archives. A few years later, in 1910, Förster-Nietzsche tasked van de Velde with designing a modest temple building in the villa's grounds, intended as a new home for the archives so she could use the villa as her private residence. Although van de Velde's design for this temple is sadly lost, we can speculate on its appearance by comparing it to other temple designs that appealed to Förster-Nietzsche at this time.

These include a sketch of a temple honouring Nietzsche by architect, Fritz Schumacher in 1898, which was widely admired, not least by Förster-Nietzsche, and a temple-monument by van de Velde that was being constructed between 1909 and 1911) in Jena to honour the scientist Ernst Abbe. Van de Velde's initial commission for a modest temple quickly evolved into a larger project when Count Harry Graf Kessler, a mutual friend of theirs and influential patron of modern art, became involved in the design. Kessler, a key figure in the avant-garde scene in Germany and Paris, was well positioned to attract wealthy sponsors for the project, although not enough to realise his ambitious vision. Under Kessler's influence, van de Velde shifted away from his original concept of a modest temple and instead focused on designing a grand temple-stadium complex in Nietzsche's honour between 1911 and 1913.

There are other buildings designed with Nietzsche in mind that are arguably less temple-like, yet still aim to evoke quasi-sacred or mystical qualities through their stylised designs or use of glass—a material often associated with transformation and transcendence. These include the often-named 'Zarathustra house' (1899–1901) at the Darmstadt Artist Colony, designed by German architect, Peter Behrens, and Behrens' *Hamburger Vorhalle* (1902), an architectural installation for the Exposition of Decorative Arts in Turin. The installation was intended to create an immersive mystical experience, simulating the interior of Zarathustra's cave, with an altar guarded by angels as its centrepiece, holding an ornate copy of *Thus Spoke Zarathustra*. Another notable example is Bruno Taut's glass monument, *Monument des Neuen Gesetzes* (1919) ('Monument to the New Law'), which features an engraved inscription from *Thus Spoke Zarathustra*.

The final building I will examine is the notorious Nietzsche Memorial Hall in Weimar (1934–44), designed by German architect Paul Schultze-Naumburg as a cultural centre for the Third Reich. The building's shell still stands today. Adolf Hitler personally contributed to the project from his private funds, although it appears to have been of ambiguous priority for him. Hitler's love of architecture is well documented; he described serving this passion 'with ardent zeal', firmly believing he would one day make a name for himself as an architect (1925/1992: 20, 34–5). His enthusiasm for architecture never waned and was directed towards his relentless ambition to construct monumental buildings that would symbolise the enduring power and legacy of the Third Reich—most notably reflected in his grandiose plans to rebuild Berlin as *Germania*, capital city of the world.

The Nietzsche Hall offers a valuable case study for understanding Hitler's perception of Nietzsche's philosophy and how much he viewed Nietzsche's legacy as a political asset. Given the unfortunate misunderstandings and misappropriations of Nietzsche's ideas, which led to their association with National Socialism, it is important to consider how architecture can reveal and evaluate the values and aspirations that shape design. Both Nietzsche and Hitler, like many others before and after, viewed architecture as a material representation of a culture's values. By exploring the kinds of building they championed and the criteria they endorsed for 'healthy' architecture, we can uncover parallels and stark contrasts in their views. Though neither articulated their architectural ideals in a straightforward manner, the differences between their positions are significant and ultimately irreconcilable.

Semper's opera house: the first Nietzsche monument?

In Chapter 4, I discussed how Semper's ideas inspired Nietzsche's understanding of the vigorous Dionysian instincts awakened during the festive atmosphere of theatrical performances. I also explored Nietzsche's early thoughts on the artistic relationship between Dionysus and Apollo, as reflected in his notes, lectures, and an essay from 1870 that served as groundwork for *The Birth of Tragedy*, published three years later in 1873. While there is no evidence that Semper ever read Nietzsche's works or that the two men met, it is noteworthy that as Nietzsche was refining his vision of Dionysus—reinterpreting the god's traditional roles, symbolism, and associations—Semper was embarking on the architectural design of the Semperoper. This project seemed to represent Dionysus in a similarly unconventional and somewhat controversial way, as though Semper sought to embody Nietzsche's Dionysus in architectural form. At this time, both men elevated Dionysus to the status of master of the arts and leader of the Muses, a role typically reserved for Apollo. The fact that they both challenged this long-standing tradition simultaneously makes the connection between Nietzsche and Semper all the more intriguing.

Apollo is typically a central figure in the ornamentation and iconography of theatre buildings and opera houses, while Dionysus (or Bacchus) appears far less frequently and with much less prominence. It is rare to see their roles reversed, yet this is precisely what Semper does with the Semperoper, and he does so boldly, making Dionysus the dominant motif both inside and outside the building. Where one would usually expect to find a statue of Apollo, Semper instead places a triumphant Dionysus with his bride, Ariadne, within a panther-drawn quadriga (a chariot drawn by four animals, usually horses) above the building's central portico and main entrance.

At the time Semper was designing this theatre, Nietzsche was making similar moves in his preparatory writings for *The Birth of Tragedy*, elevating Dionysus to a central position by associating him with the ecstatic power of music and making him the heart of tragic performances. Nietzsche's interpretation, however, was widely ridiculed and criticised within the academic community, particularly for his association of Dionysus with music and his disregard for the traditional scholarly and textual evidence from ancient Greek sources. One scathing attack by a philologist argued that Nietzsche's erroneous portrayal of Dionysus among the Muses was so misguided that it warranted his immediate dismissal from his university position!

The Semperoper gives Dionysus prominence through its ornamentation, especially in its dynamic, sculptural centrepiece. The chariot drawn by panthers in full stride creates a sense of motion, as if ready to leap from the building, carrying Dionysus and Ariadne on a flying journey through the city. Dionysus leans towards Ariadne, her veil billowing, while the ribbons of his staff flap in the wind, adding a sense of energy. This lively sculpture contrasts with the otherwise calm 'Apollonian' architectural design.

The building exemplifies an eclectic historicist style, blending Renaissance, Baroque, and Classical revival elements. Constructed from sandstone, typical of Dresden architecture from this period, the Semperoper is organised around a traditional horseshoe-shaped auditorium and features a grand marble staircase leading from the entrance to various levels. Its exterior is dominated by a prominent portico with a triangular pediment supported by Corinthian columns, adorned with sculptures and reliefs of artists, composers, dramatists, and allegorical motifs. These columns emphasise verticality, drawing the eye to the central dome above the auditorium, enhancing the building's temple-like appearance and sense of majesty.

On either side of the entrance, the symmetrical façade is marked by rhythmic arched windows, columns, pilasters, and rich ornamental carvings. Inside, the Dionysus theme continues with ceiling paintings in the upper circular foyer depicting scenes from the god's life—his upbringing by the nymphs of Nysa, the discovery of Ariadne, his punishment of the Tyrrhenian pirates, and his dismemberment by the Titans. The central painting portrays Dionysus' rebirth. Semper described the ceiling as having 'a festive effect' (Magirius, 1987: 92), a sentiment echoed by Johannes Schilling, the designer of the Dionysus and Ariadne sculpture, who said it represented 'a festive entry among the people', bringing them 'enthusiasm and joy' (Stephan, 1996: 98).

It is unlikely that Nietzsche ever visited the Semperoper, as he is believed not to have returned to Dresden after 1869. While the rhythmic symmetry of its façade might have tempered the building's opulent ornamentation and eclectic mix of historical styles in Nietzsche's eyes, Neumeyer suggests that the mere fact that 'someone had dared to lay an entire city at the feet of Dionysus and his panthers' while Nietzsche was developing his ideas for *The Birth of Tragedy*, would probably 'have given Nietzsche a solemn feeling of confirmation' of his philosophical beliefs (2001/2004: 124).

A few historians have drawn connections between the Semperoper and Nietzsche's book by suggesting that the book may have inspired the building's design. However, when considering an architectural work, it is important to do so in the context of the architect's broader portfolio of designs. When we compare the Semperoper with Semper's earlier theatre designs, it becomes evident that Dionysus is a recurring motif. For example, his designs for theatres in Rio de Janeiro (1858) and the Festspielhaus for Wagner in Munich (1864–9) both featured plans for a large sculpture of Dionysus in a carriage prominently placed above the main entrance. Similarly, Semper noted that the painted ceiling of the Semperoper, depicting scenes from the life of Dionysus, 'corresponds exactly' to the ceiling of its predecessor, which had been destroyed by fire (Magirius, 1987: 92).

Semper's interest in Dionysus predated Nietzsche's work. In fact, Nietzsche may have been familiar with the Dionysian imagery in the first Dresden theatre, as he visited it eight months before it was destroyed, to attend Dresden's premier of Wagner's *Die Meistersinger* in January 1869. While Nietzsche does not detail the building's architecture, it likely served as a striking backdrop to his profoundly positive experience of the performance—an evening he remembers as one where he felt deeply at home, both in his surroundings and within himself (Letter to Erwin Rohde; KSB.2.625: 379).

We may never understand how much Semper and Nietzsche influenced each other in their portrayals of Dionysus. It seems most likely that they were independently inspired by a shared source—an ancient tradition that directly linked Dionysus to music and the Muses, but that had largely faded from memory since the sixth century. Semper himself made reference to this tradition in a letter to sculptor Ernst Julius Hähnels (1811–91), who taught Johannes Schilling, stating, 'According to a very ancient mythological account, the Muses belong to the immediate entourage, and as it were, the court of Dionysus' (Magirius, 1987: 144). Similarly, when Nietzsche faced harsh criticism from Wilamowitz-Möellendorf for *The Birth of Tragedy*, he urged his friend Erwin Rohde to write a counter-response, citing this ancient tradition to correct the assumption that Nietzsche had made a grave error (Rohde, 1872).

Nietzsche temples

I previously noted that the most common architectural tribute to Nietzsche is the secular temple, which was intended to embody his call for a new, more creative and affirmative way of life grounded in the will to power. Although

<u>Nietzsche made it clear that he would have rejected any building erected in his name, especially one that professed to be sacred or holy, several designs I discuss here seem to have disregarded his position and would likely have drawn his ire.</u>

Many of these designs aim to lead visitors into quasi-mystical experiences, encouraging a deep reverence for Nietzsche and his philosophy through meditative walks. These walks are guided by symbolic motifs and stylised ornaments, such as sculptures and engravings, intended to prompt reflection on specific themes from his works, especially *Thus Spoke Zarathustra*.

Examples include the 'Philosopher's Walkway' in Schultze-Naumburg's Nietzsche Hall, Behrens' immersive experience of Zarathustra's dark cave, the tree-lined pathway to the Nietzsche temple designed by van de Velde and Kessler meant to evoke a sacred grove, and Schumacher's temple with its vast staircase. Arguably, these designs draw from Nietzsche's own belief in the power of walking to inspire ideas. However, the objects used to guide visitors' attention—such as quotations from Nietzsche's writings, a physical copy of *Thus Spoke Zarathustra* displayed on an altar, or statues of Apollo, Dionysus, Zarathustra, and even Nietzsche himself—seem, through their specificity, to contradict Nietzsche's call for places that encourage self-reflection, rather than offering distractions that draw attention to themselves.

While Nietzsche was incapacitated under the care of his sister, Elisabeth, and in the years following his death, she dedicated her efforts to shaping his image as a secular saint. She would dress him in a white pleated robe, reminiscent of those worn by Brahmin priests, and after he died, she sought to cement his legacy by establishing a pilgrimage site for his followers, one that could rival Wagner's Festspielhaus in Bayreuth. To achieve this, she envisioned constructing a temple-like building near to Villa Silberblick, where Nietzsche's admirers could visit his archives and be close to the place of his final moments. Efforts to design such a structure after Nietzsche's death were probably influenced by Elisabeth's efforts to portray him as saintly figure.

Fritz Schumacher's temple (1898)

It is probable that Elisabeth Förster-Nietzsche initially envisioned a temple similar to a design by German architect Fritz Schumacher called the 'Nietzsche monument. Temple of Life' ('Nietzsche-Denkmal. Tempel des Lebens'), which he sketched in 1898, two years before Nietzsche's death (Figure 4). This sketch was part of a series of 20 designs for monuments and sacred or secular buildings. Schumacher's design attracted significant attention from those involved in the Nietzsche archive, notably, Förster-Nietzsche herself, who, according to Schumacher, valued the design so much that she invited him to visit her at Villa Silberblick to discuss reconstructing it on site (1935/1949: 250). Paul Kühn, the author of the official guide to van de Velde's renovation of Villa Silberblick, believed that Schumacher's design captured the rich inner life of Nietzsche's

Figure 4 Nietzsche-Denkmal. Tempel des Lebens/Temple of Life (1898, Fritz Schumacher). Charcoal sketch.

personality and offered artistic clarification of Nietzsche's spirit (1899: 223). Additionally, Arthur Seidl, an editor working at the Nietzsche archive and involved in raising funds for a building to honour Nietzsche (which Seidl referred to as a 'Nietzsche museum' and 'artistic place of worship'), praised Schumacher's design, describing it as 'ingenious' (1901: 398–9).

Schumacher described his design as a 'quiet round temple in a lonely plateau', but the sketch suggests a structure far from passive. It conveys a sense of movement and aspiration for height, symbolised by a solitary, robed figure—perhaps a priest—cautiously ascending the dark, imposing staircase towards the temple. Atop the temple stands a towering statue, which Schumacher identified as a 'human genius' who 'rises' and 'longs to stretch its arms' ever higher. This figure is accompanied by two eagles (Zarathustra's eagle, perhaps), poised to take flight. In stark contrast, below this figure are equally large statues of 'dark giants', which are bound and subdued, their heads lowered in resignation. These giants stand at the end of two walls enclosing the central staircase, symbolising a state of enslavement (Schumacher, 1935/1949: 250).

The contrast between the statues represents the opposition between master and slave, the will to power and the will to truth. The robed figure ascending the stairs can be seen as transitioning between these states, gradually becoming more confident on their journey upwards. Seidl noted that the staircase produces a 'peculiar artistic effect', inspiring reverence and a sense of the sacred (1901: 397–8). Its enclosed design ensures that the climber's focus is solely on their ascent and the figure of the 'genius' looming above. At the bottom of the staircase, the climber is 'greeted' by 'slave people' bound by morality. As we ascend, 'our gaze passes a mysterious sphinx in front of the pillared hall' before arriving at the 'high man', who appears both 'solemn' and 'lonely', yet delighted by the horizon and vast surroundings before him (1901: 397–8). Historian Colin Trodd interprets the figure at the temple's summit as the 'ecstatic Zarathustra, a heliotropic hero emerging from a sea of darkness', with the temple itself evoking 'solitude, inner reality, and revelation' (2018: 27).

Schumacher seems to have designed the building to encourage a spiritual awakening, guiding visitors on a dramatic, introspective climb upwards. The sculptural figures along the way are meant to inspire and educate those who traverse it.

Henry van de Velde's temples (1909–13)

Although Elisabeth Förster-Nietzsche and others involved with the Nietzsche archive were enamoured with Schumacher's temple sketch, no official commission to build a replica was issued. Instead, in January 1911, Henry van de Velde accepted a commission from Förster-Nietzsche to design a 'modest' temple on land she planned to purchase below Villa Silberblick. Soon after, Förster-Nietzsche invited Harry Graf Kessler to join the project, probably hoping to leverage his political influence to secure additional funding. Kessler, familiar with Nietzsche's work, agreed to participate on the condition that the temple be expanded and made more impressive. Under his direction, the architectural designs grew increasingly elaborate, eventually evolving into designs for a temple and sports stadium resembling the Panathenaic Stadium in Athens. The projected cost for the project exceeded two million marks (equivalent to approximately £14.5 million sterling or 18–19 million US dollars in 2025, according to historical purchasing power).

Kessler envisioned a horseshoe-shaped stadium and open-air swimming pool behind a temple, connected by a colonnaded pathway. Three ceremonial tree-lined pathways, 500–800 metres long, would lead visitors to the site. Kessler explained to a sceptical Förster-Nietzsche and a hesitant van de Velde that the purpose of the stadium was to celebrate Nietzsche's teachings on 'joy in one's body', 'physical strength and beauty', and the connection between spirit, 'physical culture, force, and grace' (Easton, 2006: 187). He imagined the temple-stadium complex as a place for mass pilgrimage and gatherings, accommodating 50,000 people. Nietzsche scholar Günther Stamm noted that 'the initiated elite' would experience 'constant and emotional renewal' in the temple, while 'masses of young people' would celebrate 'the beauty of vigor and force' through athletic competitions in the stadium, all 'in the name of

Nietzsche' (Stamm, 1973–5: 314). The selected site was located on a hill in southwest Weimar, now situated between Berkaer Straße and the aptly named Henry-van-de-Velde-Straße. Today it houses a carpark and, somewhat ironically, a fitness centre as well.

Förster-Nietzsche and van de Velde were dissatisfied with Kessler's plans and preferred van de Velde's original design. Due to escalating costs and the length of time it took to finalise the design, the temple was never constructed.

<u>Had Förster-Nietzsche adhered to her original vision and accepted van de Velde's design without Kessler's involvement, a relatively modest temple would probably be standing today, in harmonious alignment with Villa Silberblick.</u>

Unfortunately, van de Velde's plans for this temple have been lost. However, I think we can get an idea of what it might have looked like by examining similar temple-like structures he designed during his renovations of Villa Silberblick, as the temple was meant to complement the villa as its close neighbour. In particular, and aside from the series of designs created at Kessler's request, it is worth considering various design elements from van de Velde's memorial building in Jena, dedicated to the scientist, Ernst Abbe (1909–11). This modest temple-like building, admired by Förster-Nietzsche, was under construction around the time van de Velde was formulating his original plans for the Nietzsche temple.

As I discussed in Chapter 4, van de Velde's designs are characterised by his use of smooth, flowing lines and his incorporation of organic materials to highlight their natural qualities. He described the effect he aimed for as 'line force', which is to say, he sought to imbue his designs with a dynamic energy that evoked uplifting sensations of movement, even dance, in the viewer. Van de Velde's Abbe memorial and his renovations for Villa Silberblick have been interpreted as examples of empowering architecture, where decorative elements seamlessly blend with the structure, imparting a sense of solidity, endurance, and reverence, while also maintaining a sense of playfulness in tribute to the figures they commemorate.

The Abbe memorial is octagonal in shape, with interior walls curving inwards to create a circular space (Figure 5). Its exterior is a solid mass of stone, uniform on all sides, intersected by four portals, each featuring a large copper-coloured door. Flanking these portals are three-quarter pillars that provide a distinction between the vertical walls and a simple, low-rising crowning cap with a glass skylight. The blend of traditional and modern materials—stone and glass—symbolises Abbe's scientific ideas, rooted in tradition yet aspiring toward future discoveries. Van de Velde frequently incorporates stylised motifs inspired by natural forms, enhancing the fluid, curvilinear shapes of his building façades. On the Abbe memorial, the pillars feature four recessed lancet shapes, giving the building the appearance of a large ribcage. These upward-pointing lancet shapes create the impression that the heavy building is striving to lift itself skywards.

In his renovations for Villa Silberblick, van de Velde used materials playfully to highlight contrasts in their textures, shapes, and natural colours (Figure 6). The combination of brick, sandstone, and white stucco plaster, and the variety of curves and right-angles, creates a lively, textured surface that is both tactile and visually striking. An imposing two-storey porch supports a horizontal, rectangular strip of red sandstone that cuts across the width of the façade, engraved with 'NIETZSCHE-ARCHIV'. This strip is flanked by two thinner vertical strips of red sandstone that rise upwards to frame two large square windows on the upper storey, bordered by white plaster. The geometric right-angled design on the upper storey is interrupted on the lower level by a curved brown wooden archway, emphasising the main entrance. A large oak door completes the top of the arch, and its curve intersects the frames of two side windows. The combination of the large arch and the vertical red strips draw the eye upwards, evoking the image of a rising sun—a motif associated with Zarathustra.

There are notable similarities in several design elements used by van de Velde for the Abbe memorial, Villa Silberblick, and one of the Nietzsche temple designs for Kessler—believed to be the third of four proposed for their project (Figure 7). Perhaps most striking is the resemblance between the solid, compact shapes of the Nietzsche temple and the Abbe memorial, both incorporating pillars and lancet shapes beneath a low-rising crowning cap. While there are clear differences, such as the elevated base of the temple to accommodate its additional storey, the similarities remain strong. Additionally, the way in which the main room of Villa Silberblick echoes the lancet shapes seen on the exteriors of both the Abbe memorial and temple is particularly interesting. Vertical wooden strips in the corners of the room, along with cavetto plaster moulding with evenly spaced grooves, mimic these shapes (Figure 8). The wooden strips divide the walls and bend to follow the curvature of the moulding, stopping just before the plain ceiling, creating an impression of greater height. The grooves enhance this effect by playing with light and shadow. Similarly, the lancet shapes of the Abbe memorial point upwards, merging with the curvature of the wall, which billow outward at the base. It is as though this interior feature of the villa mirrors the exterior of the Abbe memorial, but flipped upside down. Van de Velde's habit of incorporating interior features of one building into the exterior of another, and vice versa, would later become a point of frustration for Kessler during their work on a Nietzsche monument.

Figure 5 Ernst Abbe-Denkmal, Jena (built 1908–11, Henry van de Velde). Exterior view from the south. Author's photograph.

Figure 6 Villa Silberblick, Nietzsche-Archiv building, Weimar (renovations 1902–3, Henry van de Velde). Front elevation. Author's photograph.

Figure 7 Nietzsche temple design for Weimar (1912, Henry van de Velde). Third design. Perspective sketch. Collection ENSAV—La Cambre, Bruxelles, inv.1508. © Henry van de Velde.

Figure 8 Villa Silberblick, Weimar. Nietzsche-Archiv main room with Nietzsche herm (1905, Max Klinger). Detailing vertical wooden strips and cavetto moulding by Henry van de Velde. Author's photograph.

Van de Velde aimed to achieve a *Gesamtkunstwerk*, or a 'total work of art', where various art forms combine to create a unified and comprehensive architectural design. This concept emphasises the seamless integration of exterior and interior elements, as seen in Villa Silberblick, where the geometric play of right-angled forms continues into the wooden cladding of the entrance hall and in a stencilled frieze that links the cloakroom to a wide staircase and upper floor. The idea also extends to the fusion of architecture with sculpture and often-overlooked details like the interior fittings and furnishings, which van de Velde carefully considered in the villa's design. The warm tones of the red sandstone and white plaster on the exterior are repeated using natural wood, brass fittings—including a large brass 'N' motif above the fireplace—and red fabrics, all set against stark white ceilings.

A common feature of the Abbe memorial, Villa Silberblick, and the planed Nietzsche temple was the inclusion of a marble herm (a rectangular pillar topped with a carved head) dedicated to the man honoured by the building. Designed by renowned German artist Max Klinger (1857–1920), these herms were not placed within their building as an appendage or afterthought, but integral to the architecture, and positioned to benefit from natural light. In the Abbe memorial, when the four large doors are opened, each entrance provides a unique view of the Ernst Abbe herm, while a skylight creates dynamic shadows that seem to animate it. On bright days, the light spotlights the herm, giving it an almost mystical aura. Similarly, the Nietzsche herm in Villa Silberblick stands in natural light at the west end of the main room, in front of three windows, raised on a wooden platform. Two vertical windows flank the herm, mirroring the height of the stele, while a horizontal window frames the bust's head. Kessler had a similar vision for a Nietzsche herm in his temple, with the sculpture positioned at the back of the space on a stage resembling an altar, illuminated by side windows and a large window above the main entrance.

Despite their prominence, van de Velde found the inclusion of these herms problematic. He believed that the ideas of Nietzsche and Abbe were better represented though abstract forms than through effigies of their likeness, and that these sculptures disrupted the overall aesthetic of his designs. He felt the Nietzsche herm, standing at 2.38 metres, overpowered the room at the Nietzsche archive, while the Abbe herm, in his view, was too large and overly ornate. In both cases, he believed that the excessive emphasis on the sculptural elements created an imbalance in his *Gesamtkunstwerk*, detracting from the harmonious 'rhythm of the whole' design (van de Velde, 1995: 302).

Van de Velde was frustrated with Kessler's desire to emphasise the sculptural elements in the design of the Nietzsche temple. To van de Velde, it was an unnecessary addition to the design and had become a distraction, taking attention away from the architecture's impact. Kessler, in turn, grew frustrated with van de Velde's approach, and towards the end of the project, he began to doubt the architect's ability to create a building that could adequately reflect the 'heroism and joy' that he believed were central to Nietzsche's works. Eventually, Kessler suggested that van de Velde shift his focus to designing a 'platform as a background for the statue' that Kessler wanted to showcase: a sculpture of a young Apollo by French artist, Aristide Maillol (Kessler, 2011: 571–2).

Before arriving at the version of the temple reminiscent of the Abbe memorial that I described above and depicted in Figure 7—which Kessler rejected for its 'oppressively heavy and empty effect' and its 'complicated articulation' (Kessler, 2011: 588)—van de Velde had designed two earlier versions. His increasing frustration, and probable disillusionment with the project, eventually led him to a design that Kessler finally accepted. The first of his designs for Kessler was in the style of a classical Greek temple, resembling the Doric second temple of Hera at Paestum, Italy, that he had positioned behind the Apollo statue and was reached via a tree-lined walkway. While the classical design contradicted Nietzsche's aversion to replicating historical styles, van de Velde may have been inspired by Nietzsche's own account of feeling uplifted by the Greek spirit during a visit to the temple at Paestum—an experience I discussed in Chapter 4. Kessler recommended modifications to this initial design and van de Velde's second temple concept presented an idiosyncratic, curvaceous interpretation of a classical temple. However, Kessler criticised this version as well, arguing that it lacked a sense of monumentality and resembled a 'municipal museum', with 'gossipy forms'.

After van de Velde's second design attempt, Kessler gave him nearly impossible instructions for improvement, asking for a temple that would translate 'Nietzsche's personality into a grand architectural formula'. Kessler wanted the design to reflect 'the physiognomy of Nietzsche himself, with his formidable

Bismarckian bone structure beneath the exquisitely delicate Greek surfaces of his brow and mouth'. He added,

> I would like not only joy but almost irony in the monumental expression of this opposition, the triumph of finesse over force. A complete orchestration of these two motifs leading to a joy and serenity, an almost ironic purity and lightness.
>
> (Kessler, 2011: 573–4)

Van de Velde certainly had his work cut out, and his inevitable inability to meet these demands led Kessler to express his disappointment. Kessler lamented,

> The truth [is] our age lacks any tradition and handle on decorative architecture. This complete failure of van de Velde, after repeated efforts, to find an architectural expression for a pure and aimless joy in life and lightness proves it.
>
> (2011: 588)

The final design that was agreed upon has the heaviest aesthetic of all the temples van de Velde created for the project (Figure 9). It resembles more of a neo-Romanesque mausoleum or monument to the dead than a place of lightness and joy. The structure is a solid, impenetrable stone mass with a square plan and prominent circular features. Large arches rise on each side of its austere base, dominating the upper façade. These arches are echoed by a relatively small, bulbous dome that caps the building. The rounded forms continue in the large circular, recessed windows, which are framed by the heavy archways and serve as focal points of the design. These windows rest on rows of elongated vertical columns that stretch upwards to meet the curve of each window, forming a striated recessed wall on each side reminiscent of the 'ribcage' of the Abbe memorial.

Figure 9 Nietzsche temple design for Weimar (1912, Henry van de Velde). Final design. Perspective sketch. Collection ENSAV—La Cambre, Bruxelles, inv.1508. © Henry van de Velde.

The circular windows and 'ribs' of the walls are flanked by thick pillars that protrude from each corner, drawing together the archways on either side. The pillars feature a central groove that runs their full length, extending the ribcage pattern, and each pillar ends in a massive stone plinth. These plinths are the same height as the central portal, and each side of the square blocks of stone is punctuated by a relatively small circular window. The main portal is nestled between two of these corner plinths and sits beneath a triangular pediment, which rests on two columns, which are adorned with a simple curved motif at their tops. This motif is repeated in the stone walls encasing the six steps leading up to the entrance.

Ironically, earlier in the project, Kessler remarked, 'heaviness is what Nietzsche hated most in life!' (Kessler and van de Velde 2015: 578). Given this, it is doubtful that this design would have received Nietzsche's—or Zarathustra's—approval.

Building with glass and crystal: Bruno Taut and Peter Behrens

Many temples or monuments dedicated to Nietzsche have used natural light to highlight specific interior spaces. Carefully positioned windows direct visitors' attention to these focal points, which often showcase an object associated with Nietzsche. When illuminated, objects or spaces can often induce feelings of reverence or awe, as if spotlit by other-worldly forces. Glass plays a crucial role in creating this effect. Historically, glass has been associated with spirituality due to its transparent or translucent qualities, symbolising transcendence and transformation. Its ability to reflect light also evokes metaphors of connections between material and immaterial worlds, of divine light passing into the earthly realm. The symbolism of glass and crystal frequently appears in artistic depictions of Zarathustra's teachings, notably in architectural designs of Peter Behrens and Bruno Taut.

The allusion to Zarathustra's crystal, precious stone, or diamond, is arguably overemphasised within artistic circles devoted to Nietzsche, as this motif does not play a prominent role in Zarathustra's teachings or in *Thus Spoke Zarathustra* more broadly. When it does appear, its mention is brief and loosely related to themes of artistic creativity, rebirth, and willpower. For example, Zarathustra calls upon women to become 'a plaything, pure and fine, like a precious stone, illumined by the virtues of a world that is not yet here [...] Let your hope be: "May I give birth to the Superman!"' (Z.I.18: 92). On another occasion, Zarathustra urges his brothers to *become hard* like diamonds, because 'creators are hard', unyielding and resistant (Z.III.12[29]: 231).

Peter Behrens incorporated stylised motifs of a diamond and an eagle throughout a house he designed for the Darmstadt Artist Colony (1901). This has led some critics and analysts to describe the building as 'Zarathustra's house' or a building designed in 'Zarathustra's style'. Behrens was a founding member of the Deutscher Werkbund, a teacher to notable architects of the modern era—such as Le Corbusier, Walter Gropius, Ludwig Mies van der Rohe, and Bruno Taut—and an admirer of Nietzsche. He once expressed to Förster-Nietzsche that visiting her at Villa Silberblick fulfilled a long-held wish, allowing him to express 'all my veneration and my deepest admiration for the Wise Artist' (Buddensieg, 1980: 40).

Opinions are divided on whether Behrens' house reflects the kind of creative renewal or rebirth implied by Zarathustra's crystal. Some view its prominent gables and contrasting patterned bands of masonry as fairly ordinary, and characteristic of Northern German vernacular architecture, with a conventional interior layout. Others see it as a deliberate attempt at novelty and a curious architectural experiment.

Behrens extended the crystalline theme in his interior design, *Hamburger Vorhalle*, for the German section of the first International Exposition of Modern Decorative Arts in Turin in 1902 (Figure 10). Here, he more openly experimented with Zarathustrian imagery, explicitly linking Nietzsche's philosophy to Germany's aspirations for a new, powerful, artistic culture and industry. The design featured a dark, cool chamber with stucco walls and a ceiling shaped like stalactites, evoking the sense of a mysterious cave—specifically, Zarathustra's cave. Its focal point was a large copy of *Thus Spoke Zarathustra*, bound in a cover adorned with a stylised crystal image. The book was displayed on a plinth within a square area, guarded by two angelic figures whose wings enclose the space in reverence. The book was positioned on its altar beneath a shaft of light, directed into the room through a coloured glass skylight. The *Hamburger Vorhalle* received mixed reviews and was mockingly referred to by some as the 'grave of the unknown Superman'.

Figure 10 Hamburger Vorhalle, Exposition of the Decorative Arts, Turin (built 1902, Peter Behrens). © Bildarchiv Foto Marburg.

Bruno Taut developed the symbolism of crystal and glass far beyond decorative elements, designing houses and even entire towns made almost entirely of glass. Taut, having read *Thus Spoke Zarathustra*, described it to his brother Max (also an architect) as 'a book of enormous and serious vitality' from which he had learnt a great deal (Whyte, 1982: 85, n.19). Sadly, he did not elaborate on what he had learnt, leaving the extent of Nietzsche's influence on his architectural ideas unclear. The work by Taut most often linked to Nietzsche is his visionary book, *Alpine Architektur des Architekten* (1919), within which he imagines vast crystalline structures, designed as dwellings for artists, embedded into mountains, gorges, and geometricised natural formations. These glass temples, pyramids, cathedrals, domes, and more—interspersed with waterfalls of red glass, balconies, and crystal-lined caves—were meant to provide spaces for artists to reflect on their relationships with one another and their environments. Taut envisioned his glass architecture as harnessing sunlight to enhance the physical and spiritual qualities of the glass, in turn, inspiring the artistic communities living in these remote, artistic havens away from the humdrum of conventional cities.

It is difficult to imagine Nietzsche approving of turning natural mountain landscapes into glittering palaces and to cityscapes more suited to fantasy fiction than modern German life. While Taut included annotations alongside his drawings, he did not fully explain his intentions. The final image in the series appears to invite readers to reflect on progressive stages of unreality. It depicts a cloud-like shape of dotted lines, containing the words, 'Sterne Welten. Schlaf. Tod. Das Grosse Nichts. Das Namenlose.' ('Star worlds. Sleep. Death. Immensity. Nothingness. Namelessness.') Beneath this, a single word appears: 'Ende.' ('The End.'). Though Nietzsche is not mentioned in the annotations, some commentators have tenuously linked *Alpine Architektur* to Nietzsche by suggesting that its imagined inhabitants are Nietzschean artists or merely referencing Nietzsche's love of icy mountain peaks.

A more convincing connection between Taut and Nietzsche can be found in another of Taut's works, a sketch for the *Monument des Neuen Gesetzes* (1919), or 'Monument to the New Law', which directly referenced Nietzsche. A quotation from the chapter, 'Of Old and New Laws' in *Thus Spoke Zarathustra* is engraved into the glass of this monument, which was sketched in the same year that *Alpine Architektur* was published (Figure 11).

<u>Interestingly, the sketch for the monument begins with the same phrase that ends *Alpine Architektur*, suggesting that 'Nothingness' and 'Death' signify not the 'End' of life, but rather a transformation, in line with Nietzsche's understanding of nihilism or death as a prelude to a rebirth.</u>

The 'Monument to the New Law' was intended to symbolise a society at the brink of change—a marker of endings, the loss of meaning, and death, particularly as a memorial for those who died in the Great War and of the dissolution of political state rule. At the same time, it heralded new beginnings and the promise of cultural renewal, embodying Nietzsche's concept of the revaluation of values.

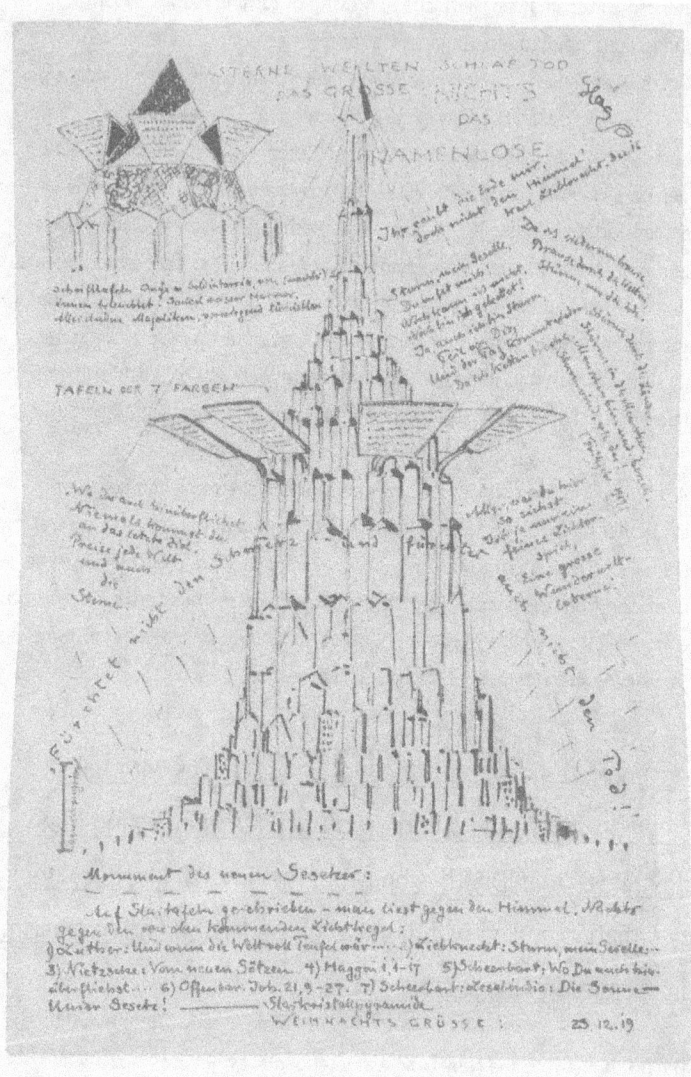

Figure 11 Monument des Neuen Gesetzes (1919, Bruno Taut). Illustrated letter with a drawing of a project for the Monument to the Dead. © Canadian Center for Architecture.

The monument is pyramid-shaped, constructed from glass prisms that slot together to suggest a large crystal pointing towards the sky. Its tip shaped like an arrow with a star-shaped base, perhaps alluding to 'Sterne Welten' (Star worlds). Taut's sketch depicts rays of light reflecting downwards from the tip towards seven raised, multicoloured panels positioned at mid-height, fanning outwards and upwards. According to Taut's handwritten notes below the sketch, the building is clad in turquoise blue majolica with a white marble base, and the panels are made of onyx with gold inlay.

The panels are inscribed with quotations that can be easily read at ground level in the natural light of day, and at night through artificial lighting. Taut briefly mentions his choice of quotations:

> (1) Luther: And were this world all devils ... 2) Liebknecht: Storm, my companion ... 3) Nietzsche: Of the new idol 4) Haggai 1, 1–17 5) Scheerbart: Wherever you flee ... 6) Revelation Joh.21, 9–27 7) Scheerbart: Lesabéndio: The sun—our law!)

The passage Taut selected from Nietzsche is a lengthy section in which Zarathustra condemns the state as a powerful adversary and urges us to look beyond it to 'the rainbow and bridges to the Superman'. Perhaps Taut intended his glass monument to evoke a portal or bridge to the Superman through the play of kaleidoscopic lights from the monument's colourful panels.

Nietzsche and Nazism

Aside from van de Velde's renovations at Villa Silberblick in Weimar, another notable building honouring Nietzsche stands today, albeit in a partially derelict state. This is the Nietzsche Hall, constructed next to Villa Silberblick, designed to serve as a cultural centre and site of pilgrimage for National Socialism. Before discussing this building, it is important to contextualise the relationship between Nietzsche's philosophy and Nazi ideology.

Nietzsche's relationship to National Socialism is complex and often misunderstood. Nietzsche had died long before the rise of National Socialism, yet his ideas were manipulated posthumously to align more closely with Nazi ideology, providing a veneer of philosophical support for some of its principles. This association did not originate with Hitler—who is believed to have never read Nietzsche's works—but largely through the editorial influence of Elisabeth Förster-Nietzsche, Nietzsche's sister. She published *The Will to Power* under Nietzsche's name, which contributed to the distortion of his ideas. Two Nazi ideologues, Alfred Rosenberg (1893–1946) and Alfred Bäumler (1887–1968), also played significant roles in this reinterpretation, endorsing *The Will to Power* as Nietzsche's most significant work, and promoting a skewed version of Nietzsche's concept of the will to power as his central message.

Nazi propaganda was rooted in the völkisch myth, which drew on Aryan and Nordic paganism, presenting the German people as an idealised community. Central to this myth was a mystical connection between the German race and the natural world. In his influential work, *Nazi Ideology: The Myth of the Twentieth Century* (1930), Rosenberg argued that German people had lost their identity due to the corrupting influence of Jewish people, who promoted a competing myth that cast themselves as the 'chosen' ones destined to inherit the world. He blamed the Jewish people's materialistic outlook (along with the proletariat and the bourgeoisie) for Germany's rapid industrialisation at the turn of the twentieth century, which he believed had led the German people astray from their true nature.

Rosenberg called for political action to reclaim German racial authority, urging the people to embrace values of will, honour, and discipline to usher in a new heroic era for Germany. In a lecture delivered at the Nietzsche archive in Villa Silberblick in 1944, commemorating Nietzsche's centenary, Rosenberg portrayed Nietzsche as a philosopher of war and crisis, and Zarathustra as a warrior—both as symbolic figureheads who could help the Nazis overcome their struggles in the face of critical war by reclaiming myth and power for the German *Volk*.

Bäumler similarly misrepresented Nietzsche, asserting that his philosophy endorsed the superiority of Nordic-Germanic races and denigrated the Jewish race. He portrayed Zarathustra as a prophet of Nazi ideology, fighting for the rights of the *Volk*. In Bäumler's reading, the individual's struggle became the collective struggle of the German people, which could be overcome through the exercise of the will to power. He politicised this concept, framing it as the German people's will to fulfil their destiny and claim their inherent rights. Bäumler argued that the Germans possessed a particularly strong will to power, shaped by their historical struggles. As for Nietzsche's many positive comments about the Jewish people and his criticism of German nationalism, Bäumler either ignored them or dismissed them as rhetorical strategies used by Nietzsche to provoke his German readers.

The skewed interpretations of Nietzsche that fuelled the National Socialist cultural and racial agenda often embraced a superficial understanding of the will to power. It ascribed this concept to the German people as an inherit trait, suggesting it was the means by which they could assert their natural right as a master race by overcoming all opposition, particularly from other races that promoted their own myths of power and belonging. Consequently,

<u>architecture inspired by Nazi ideas of the will to power differ substantially from architecture informed by Nietzsche's concept of the will to power.</u>

Nazi architecture

Albert Speer, Hitler's chief architect, remarked that 'at bottom, I think [Hitler's] sense of political mission and his passion for architecture were always inseparable' (1970/2009: 80). Interestingly, despite this assertion, Hitler never explicitly dictated the architectural styles the Nazis should adopt. To enhance their national appeal while gaining power, the Nazi Party tended to adopt a negative stance towards art and architectural design, denigrating styles that did not align with the völkisch myth rather than promoting their own. Designs considered too radical or expressive of other national styles were outlawed, including the internationalist designs of the Bauhaus school, which the party labelled

'Bolshevist'. This led to the closure of the school, first in Weimar in 1925, then in Dessau in 1932, and in Berlin in 1933, along with the purging of abstract and modernist artworks from public view due to their perceived 'degenerate' nature.

After 1928, the Nazi Party found itself in the challenging position of needing to establish its own cultural programme and distinctive architectural style. The outcome was a confusing and contradictory mix of styles that arguably mirrored the internal discord within the party itself. Their architectural portfolio drew from various influences, including German Romanesque buildings of the Middle Ages, the 'eternal values' of neo-classicism, regional 'folk' styles of rural Germany, and radical styles intended to signal the dawn of a new regime. Historian, Barbara Miller Lane notes the irony in the Nazi architectural programme's appropriation of 'buildings which closely resembled the work of the radical architects whom the Nazis had opposed' (1985: 9).

What emerged as a 'Nazi architectural style' was a stylistic mishmash of the kind Nietzsche sought to reject, reflecting the lack of conviction and absence of a unifying instinct that he criticised. This initial sense of style stemmed from a negative conception of power, described by Nietzsche as *'ressentiment'*, where values are not created organically but contrived in reaction to values created freely by others. This results in a 'parasitic' power—a mere semblance of power that feeds off the will to power of others, establishing values that stand in stark opposition to those freely created. These negative values are then weaponised to undermine the freedom and creativity of others.

According to Speer, Hitler had no specific architectural style in mind for the Third Reich. Speer stated:

> What was branded as the official architecture of the Reich was only the neoclassicism transmitted by [Ludwig] Troost; it was multiplied, altered, exaggerated, and sometimes distorted to the point of ludicrousness [...] it would be a mistake to try to look within Hitler's mentality for some ideologically based architectural style.
>
> (1970/2009: 42–3)

Despite this lack of a defined style, Hitler outlined general principles for Nazi architecture in his cultural speech, *Kunst und Politik* (*Art and Politics*), presented at the seventh National Socialist Congress in Nuremberg on 11 September 1935. He expressed his intent to revive the nation's creative powers through a new, great architecture, although he did not provide specific details of what this would entail.

Hitler emphasised that great architecture required an 'authoritarian will'. In contrast to Nietzsche's approach, this will emanated from the state—a totalitarian force intended to be exalted through architecture that represented the 'community'. From Zarathustra's perspective, this authoritarian will is a depraved force, characterised as the 'coldest of cold monsters' (a viewpoint shared by Bruno Taut, who sought to inscribe Zarathustra's words onto his 'Monument des Neuen Gesetzes'). Hitler also believed that great architecture should embody 'heroism', but his interpretation diverged significantly from Nietzsche's. For Hitler, this heroism meant constructing colossal buildings rapidly, showcasing technological innovations and experimenting with innovative methods that pushed, hurried, and accelerated the limits of talent and industry.

Furthermore, Hitler called for architecture to embody 'pure' forms—designs that are simple, consistent, and 'organic'—achievable through natural materials that align with a building's function. He claimed that such designs would convey 'clarity' and 'honesty', principles shared by Nietzsche, van de Velde, and Sullivan. However, for Hitler, 'purity' also implied a racially healthy community, free from foreign influences and reflective of the Germanic nation. He also associated purity with 'eternal values', with the use of durable construction materials like granite and marble to ensure the buildings of his empire would endure for thousands of years, symbolising its lasting power and legacy. Speer noted that Hitler 'appreciated the permanent qualities of the classical style' because he believed he found connections between the Dorians and his own Germanic heritage (1970/2009: 42). Hitler was particularly drawn to buildings featuring 'colonnades, large flat surfaces, and minimal ornamentation', components that Nietzsche valued for fostering self-reflection and silencing distracting thoughts. However, as Speer observed, these features were often 'inflated' and 'grandiose', with massive colonnades and colossal surfaces designed to keep the empire's power at the forefront of the individual's thoughts, overshadowing their personal reflections (1970/2009: 53, 138).

The stark contrast between Nazi architecture and Nietzsche's architectural preferences is perhaps best exemplified by Speer's plans for Germania, created at Hitler's request to reflect his vision of the global dominance of the Germanic empire. Speer later noted that the immense scale of this architecture 'violated the human scale', rendering it 'abnormal' (1970/2009: 138). The plans for this colossal city featured a palatial chancellery for Hitler, covering an area of 22 million square feet, and a triumphal arch soaring 400 feet high—so vast that the Arc de Triomphe in Paris could fit inside it 49 times. However, the crowning achievement of the city was the mountainous domed Volkshalle or 'People's Hall'. Designed as a sacred shrine to National Socialism and for the public adoration of Hitler, this building drew inspiration from the Pantheon of the Roman Emperor Hadrian. It boasted an 'almost inconceivable diameter' of 825 feet and a height of 726 feet (Speer, 1970/2009: 153). With a total height of 950 feet and a volume of nearly 27.5 million cubic yards (p. 154), it was so immense that when filled to capacity with 180,000 people, there were concerns it might generate its own rain clouds. Upon seeing a model of the new city, Speer's father exclaimed, 'You've all gone completely crazy' (p. 133). The architecture of Germania symbolises a power of domination, where vast, grandiose buildings dwarf and obliterate the individual.

Reconciling Nietzsche and Nazism through architecture? The case of the Nietzsche Hall

Nietzsche and Nazism are incompatible, and any effort to align the two stems from a misinterpretation of Nietzsche's philosophical ideas, particularly his concept of the will to power. Despite this, it is interesting to explore how architecture was used in an attempt to merge these ideas, as seen in the design and construction of a building meant to honour Nietzschean thought while serving as a cultural Centre for National Socialism. This building, the Nietzsche

Hall in Weimar, was designed by Nazi architect Paul Schultze-Naumburg on behalf of Hitler and Elisabeth Förster-Nietzsche.

The Nietzsche Hall offers a compelling case study to assess how deeply Hitler was invested in Nietzsche as a philosophical spokesperson for the Germanic myth that he and his associates propagated.

In analysing the Nietzsche Hall, it is helpful to set aside momentarily the fact that Nietzsche's philosophy was distorted by the Nazis and imagine the possibility that they believed they had fully understood his ideas.

The Nietzsche Hall's importance to Hitler was closely tied to his perception of Schultze-Naumburg, who was tasked with its design. Schultze-Naumburg was a founding member of the Deutscher Werkbund and served as director of the State College for Architecture and Crafts in Weimar, an institution intended to replace the Bauhaus school. His architecture was shaped by the principles of 'Blood and Soil', which he elaborated on in his book, *Kunst und Rasse* (*Art and Race*, 1928). His work often incorporated traditional German rustic 'homeland' styles. Despite his rejection of radical modernism, Schultze-Naumburg's career with the Nazi Party was marred when he criticised the growing trend of excessive monumentalism favoured by their regime, which he denounced as 'wantonly parvenu' (Kitchen, 2017: 31). His final major commission came in 1935 before he was forced into retirement from his position in Weimar, making the Nietzsche Hall his last significant architectural project.

It is often believed that Hitler chose Schultze-Naumburg as the architect for the Nietzsche Memorial Hall, but Förster-Nietzsche had a longstanding friendship with Schultze-Naumburg over several decades, and his selection may have been at her request. If Schultze-Naumburg had been Hitler's choice, it would suggest that the Nietzsche Hall was a relatively low priority for Hitler, and that Nietzsche's legacy was not a significant part of Hitler's political agenda. Had Hitler been more committed to the project, he probably would have assigned one of his more trusted architects to design the Hall, such as Albert Speer, Paul Ludwig Troost, or Hermann Giesler.

Förster-Nietzsche first met Hitler in January 1932 at the premiere of Mussolini's play, *Campo di Maggio*, at the National Theatre in Weimar. She invited Hitler to visit the Nietzsche archive at Villa Silberblick the next day, which he accepted, bringing Schultze-Naumburg along. Hitler visited Villa Silberblick on several occasions with different officials, including Albert Speer. The exact timing and origin of the idea to build a memorial hall for Nietzsche remain unclear, but if the idea came from Förster-Nietzsche, it might have revived her earlier desire—expressed 21 years earlier—to build a modest temple-like structure in honour of her brother.

What we do know is that after Hitler's visit to Villa Silberblick on 2 October 1934, he contributed 50,000 Reichsmarks from his private funds to establish a 'Nietzsche Memorial Fund' for the construction of a memorial hall next to the villa, with Schultze-Naumburg as its architect. Although Förster-Nietzsche died five years before the building's completion (with Hitler and members of his cabinet attending her funeral, a ceremony that was elevated to a level normally reserved for crown heads of state), the Hall was never used for its intended purpose.

At the outset, Hitler appeared enthusiastic about the Nietzsche Memorial Hall project, given he contributed funds from his personal finances and made an impromptu visit to Villa Silberblick in October 1935 to reassure Förster-Nietzsche personally that the building would go ahead. Notably, this visit took place just one month after Hitler delivered his speech, *Kunst und Politik*, in which he expressed his ambition to construct grand buildings to honour the 'few' German creators who had achieved 'the highest pitch of human achievement' (1935/1936: 41). These buildings, he claimed, would permanently 'imprint' the 'cultural stamp of the German race' (p. 42). While Hitler did not specify who these individuals were, his words convinced Richard Oehler, Nietzsche's cousin, that he had publicly endorsed a monument to Nietzsche. Oehler later expressed his delight to Förster-Nietzsche, praising the 'wonderful, grand speech of our dear leader' for asserting that Nietzsche, alongside Richard Wagner, ought to have great monuments built in their name to symbolise their era (GSA.72/2597).

The timing of Hitler's visit to Förster-Nietzsche, shortly after his Party Congress speech, suggests that Nietzsche may have been on Hitler's mind when he made those remarks.

Hitler's interest in the memorial hall, however, seems to wane over time. In his memoires, Albert Speer refers disparagingly to the project and its architect, noting that 'Hitler undertook to finance an annex to the old Nietzsche house', and that 'Förster-Nietzsche was willing to have Schultze-Naumburg design it'. According to Speer, Hitler commented that Schultze-Naumburg is 'better at that sort of thing, doing something in keeping with the old house'. Speer noted, Hitler 'was plainly pleased to be able to offer the architect some small sop' (1970/2009: 109).

It is telling that Hitler, who typically involved himself in the finest details of construction projects across Germany, left all decisions regarding the Nietzsche Hall to the Committee members of the Nietzsche Memorial Fund (the Nietzsche Archive Foundation, Fritz Schaukel, and Schultze-Naumburg). Presumably Hitler was preoccupied with other major building projects, such as the Gauzentrum in Weimar, designed by Hermann Giesler, which was intended as a model for the Gauforum complexes planned for every Gau capital (the governing centres of power in the Third Reich). Speer suggests that Hitler assigned the Nietzsche Hall project to Schultze-Naumburg as a consolation after the architect submitted unsuccessful designs for the Gauforum, which Hitler mocked as 'an oversized marketplace for a provincial town' before discarding them, considering Schultze-Naumburg better suited for developing 'old houses' (Speer, 1970/2009: 108).

Whatever enthusiasm Hitler initially had for the Nietzsche Hall seemed to have faded by October 1939. While other construction projects were accelerated and pushed forward, even during the early years of the War, work on the Nietzsche Hall was halted. By that time, the building's exterior was largely finished, and during the topping out ceremony on 3 August 1938 (attended by Nazi officials, such as Josef Goebbels, though not Hitler), only the hastily installed stone inscription indicated Hitler's endorsement. The inscription read: *'Friedr. Nietzsche zum Gedächtnis. Erbaut unter Adolf Hitler im VI Jahre des Dritten Reiches'* (Friedr. Nietzsche in Memory. Built Under Adolf Hitler in the 6th Year of the Third Reich).

The Nietzsche Hall, Weimar (1934–44)

The Nietzsche Hall, located at Humboldtstraße 36a, presents itself as a modest and restrained neighbour to Villa Silberblick. Its exterior is clad with dressed ashlar—uniform, rectangular blocks of stone with a limestone face—reflecting Schultze-Naumburg's disciplined and conservative approach. Its main entrance is set off from the street by a walled gate and is centrally positioned beneath an overlying cornice where the stone plaque once commemorated the building's construction. Similar to the temple-stadium complex designed by van de Velde under Kessler's guidance, the Hall was intended to feature prominent statues of Dionysus and Apollo flanking the entrance (Figure 12).

Though the building's front elevation appears smaller than it is, the Hall stretches approximately 90 metres in length and covers nearly 5,000 square metres. Entering through the stone portal leads to a one-storey cloakroom, originally planned with parquet flooring and black marble busts of Nietzsche and Hitler. This room opened into two narrow reception rooms and a long, skylit corridor, 30 metres in length, designed as a ceremonial passageway lined with busts of thinkers who inspired Nietzsche, alongside paintings related to his philosophy. Known as the 'Philosopher's Walk', the corridor aimed to provide visitors with an uplifting, spiritual experience shaped by Nietzsche's ideas, which were presented as eternally valid and rooted in revered cultural traditions.

The corridor led into a festive room, which opened into a larger one. At the far end, a semicircular apse was intended to house a large statue of Nietzsche or Zarathustra, positioned to dominate the walker's line of sight and serve as the focal point of the journey. The first festive room, accessible from the corridor, could accommodate 200 people and was intended for lectures and meetings to establish 'communities of higher men', as described by Richard Oehler (1935/1938: 13). This room featured a coffered ceiling and a high, simple French window with a rounded arch at the northern end, opening to a small balcony overlooking the garden of Villa Silberblick. A nearby glazed door led to a balustrade terrace, offering extended views of the villa and Weimar.

Figure 12 Nietzsche Memorial Hall, Weimar (built 1934–44, Paul Schultze-Naumburg). Model, with figures of Apollo and Dionysus flanking the main entrance. Photograph, January 1937. © Goethe und Schiller Archiv. Photo: Klassik Stiftung Weimar. GSA 72/2610.

Adjacent to the smaller festive room was a larger hall, nearly 8 metres high, designed to host 600 people for communal events. This hall featured floor-to-ceiling French windows leading to the terrace, but its centrepiece was the large statue. Visitors, entering through the large portal, would be greeted by Nietzsche's two gods and encouraged to walk with reverence along the corridor guided by Nietzsche's intellectual heroes, lit as if by divine light from above, with an unbroken view of the larger-than-life Nietzsche or Zarathustra statue growing larger with each step. This walk echoed the effect of Schumacher's temple, where the statue of the 'genius' looms ever closer as one ascends its staircase.

The festive wing of the building is connected to a second, two-storey wing, forming an overall horseshoe-shaped layout with a small atrium at the centre where the two wings meet. This second wing is more functional in design, housing the library, various office spaces for the Nietzsche archive, and a caretaker's apartment on the ground floor. Its utilitarian purpose is reflected in the simplicity of its design and the use of relatively inexpensive materials, such as cork flooring. The two wings differ significantly in symbolism, function, materials, and aesthetic effect, with the atrium perhaps serving as a contemplative space that unites these contrasting elements.

The ceremonial significance of the building is largely emphasised by the placement, size, and symbolic imagery of its sculptures. Without these sculptures, the Hall probably would not have featured the long corridor as its central architectural element. In this way, the Nietzsche Hall echoes a challenge that van de Velde encountered in designing buildings meant to honour great thinkers—where the sculptural programme took precedence over the architectural design itself. This issue also frustrated both van de Velde and Kessler in the planning of their temple-stadium project. The plain and simple architecture of the Hall presents itself as a backdrop for the sculptures, carefully staged and placed to evoke profound, spiritual experiences for visitors.

The design of the Hall and the selection of its sculptures suffered from a lack of clear direction from its organising committee. From the outset, the project was poorly managed, with disagreements among committee members about the building's appearance and purpose. Fritz Sauckel pushed for a grand monument with a ceremonial hall, aiming to establish it as a cultural Centre for National Socialism that would outshine all others. In contrast, Förster-Nietzsche advocated for something more modest and 'simple', in line with Villa Silberblick (GSA.72.2597).

The situation was further complicated by Nietzsche and Förster-Nietzsche's cousins, Adalbert and Richard Oehler. Adalbert disliked van de Velde's renovations of Villa Silberblick and wanted a hall that would overshadow it in grandeur, resembling the large new buildings of the National Socialist Party in Munich (GSA.72.2597). He envisioned the Hall in a 'Nordic German' style, serving as a site of 'pilgrimage' and 'sanctuary' for the masses, with Nietzschean ideas playing a secondary role. He imagined numerous Nietzschean sayings engraved into the design, highlighting ideas he believed aligned with National Socialism, such as 'advanced breeding'. Richard Oehler, on the other hand, praised the 'creative power' of van de Velde's design, which he believed made people feel 'at home', regardless of whether they adhered to Zarathustra's teachings (Oehler, 1935/1938: 12). Richard felt that the Hall's design should complement Villa Silberblick and, together with it, form a larger 'cult site' that would 'awaken creative experiences' for all visitors.

Schultze-Naumburg and his designs faced ongoing criticism from the committee members. The overall project was hindered by a lack of unifying vision—a central will to power—that could reconcile the conflicting desires and ambitions of its contributors into a cohesive and distinctive design. As Nietzsche himself maintained, the *one needful thing* is to govern and to form with 'a single taste', whether that taste is good or bad is of less consequence, so long as it is unified (GS.290). Whenever the committee disagreed with Schultze-Naumburg's evolving plans, they would often attribute it to his weak will, viewing him as incapable of mastering the creative powers required for the task. Adalbert Oehler, for instance, remarked, 'Professor Schultze-N. was once, but today is no longer the man who can create such a task [...] in accordance with the spirit of the new age' (GSA.72/2597). It took two years of planning to arrive at the final design, going through several drafts, which were described at one time or other as 'meagre', simplistic, and unworthy of Nietzsche's legacy by Sauckel, or not simple and 'solemn' enough by Förster-Nietzsche.

The sculptural programme for the Nietzsche Hall was also marred by disagreements, particularly over the theme for the central statue. Should it depict Nietzsche, Zarathustra, Dionysus and Apollo, or another motif related to Nietzsche's philosophy? These disputes persisted for years, even after Sauckel announced in January 1940 that construction on the building would be suspended indefinitely due to financial constraints. By April 1942, on the occasion of Nietzsche's 100th birthday, the idea arose to place an authentic antiquity in the apse. Benito Mussolini, an admirer of Nietzsche, responded by donating a Roman replica of a Greek statue of a clothed and bearded Dionysus by Praxiteles of Athens, which he had required illegally from the National Museum of Rome. The statue arrived at Villa Silberblick in January 1944, as Weimar was under attack from US aircraft. However, it soon became apparent that the statue was too large to fit in the Nietzsche Hall.

Conclusion: Nietzschean lessons for architects

Nietzsche asserted that 'only ideas *won by walking* have value' (TI.1: 34), and this sentiment seems to reflect the realisation and development of his own philosophical ideas, which were deeply connected to the urban and natural landscapes he enjoyed walking in. Throughout his published works, notes, and personal letters, Nietzsche made various passing comments on specific buildings and architectural designs, often expressing either admiration or disdain. While these observations are typically overlooked by scholars as minor and inconsequential details, when viewed in the broader context of his philosophy, they gain deeper significance. They offer insight into key themes of his thought, such as the rise and fall of cultural values, the transformative role of aesthetics in life, and the will to power, which fuels human creativity and imagination.

For Nietzsche, buildings were important social markers that reflected the core values of the communities that commissioned them. He believed architects carry the profound responsibility of designing structures that address the fundamental needs of these communities. This responsibility is fraught with difficulty, as the architect's role is not to cater to popular demand but to address deeper, often unrecognised needs.

In Nietzsche's philosophy, architects hold a visionary or prophetic position, with the power to shape and transform the fundamental values and cultural perspectives of entire communities.

As I mentioned in Chapter 4, architects can be regarded as forerunners to Nietzsche's figure of the Übermensch or superman, channelling the creative spirit that produced the great architectural achievements of the past and reviving it through new, innovative designs relevant to the present. Central to this is the exercise of their positive will to power—a task that requires immense self-discipline. Architects must resist the temptation to take an easier path, such as cutting corners in their designs, falling back on formulaic or derivative work, or sacrificing artistic integrity for financial gain by taking on large-scale projects that result in sterile, uniform designs—such as tract housing developments.

By mastering their instincts through the will to power, architects can create designs that are more attuned to the needs of their communities and express a unified, vital vision. Buildings designed in this way not only embody the architect's will to power but also empower those who interact with them. Thus, the architect's responsibility extends beyond the act of building; they are charged with elevating the cultural tastes and standards of the community through their work.

Nietzsche criticised the architectural standards of late nineteenth-century Germany for its overly ornate and cluttered façades, filled with eclectic decorations. He saw the decline of modern culture reflected in the excessive use of gables, turrets, and mouldings, all mixed together in a recycling of historical styles, often favouring the Gothic and Baroque. To Nietzsche, this was an inauthentic attempt to invoke the Dionysian spirit that Germany so urgently needed to foster for vitality and innovation. Modern buildings appeared superficial to him, akin to the exaggerated theatrical effects he criticised in Wagner's music.

Apart from Gottfried Semper and Alessandro Antonelli, Nietzsche regarded the architects of his time as lacking the creative genius to harness the spirit of their age. In a similar vein, Walter Gropius would later claim in 1919 that 'there are no architects today; we are all merely preparing the way for someone who will once again deserve the name of architect'. Le Corbusier offered a more nuanced assessment. While he acknowledged that in his day 'a great epoch has begun', and 'a new spirit' and 'new style' were emerging, he believed that engineers were leading this transformation, while architects lagged behind (1923/2016: 146–7). Engineering, he argued, had reached 'its full height', while architecture was in an 'unhappy state of regression'. He described engineers as 'healthy and virile, active and useful', whereas architects were 'disenchanted and idle, boastful or morose' (pp. 93–4). Despite this, many architects of the time tried to portray themselves as heroic figures whose innovative designs could secure creative success for Germany and beyond.

Several architects framed their heroic aspirations in Nietzschean terms, including Le Corbusier and Louis H. Sullivan, who saw themselves as visionary figures deeply influenced by Nietzsche's prophet, Zarathustra. It has been suggested that both men emulated Zarathustra's literary voice in their writings and even modelled their personalities after him. Architectural historian, Jean-Louis Cohen argued that *Thus Spoke Zarathustra* convinced Le Corbusier of his own 'prophetic calling' as the 'prophet of a new architecture' (1999: 317). Similarly, architectural theorist Stanislaus von Moos claimed that Le Corbusier saw himself as Nietzsche's 'lonely superman, destined to sacrifice' himself and his ideas 'for the sake of mankind' (1968/2009: 29). Architect, Charles Jencks added that Le Corbusier had 'a highly developed sense of his own destiny', drawing from 'Nietzsche's notion of the Superman' (1973: 59). Sullivan, in a similar manner, cast himself as a heroic architect, asserting that his work could 'concentrate the powers of will', 'shape character', 'make good citizens', and 'lay the foundation for a generation of real architects' (1902/2014: 226).

Architectural historian Narciso Menocal describes Sullivan's eventual disillusionment with the social and architectural trends of his time as mirroring Zarathustra's tragic disposition, both becoming 'prophets without an audience', stifled by a society that rejected their values (Menocal, 1981: 89, 100). David Van Zanten, another architectural historian, supports this view, describing Sullivan as a 'strange, great, solitary figure', isolated in his office at the top of the Auditorium Tower (Van Zanten, 2000: 7)—a symbolic retreat reminiscent, perhaps, of Zarathustra's cave high up in the mountains.

Such lofty and heroic views of oneself can give rise to a dangerous form of egoism, especially when the desire to engage with the spirit of the times turns into a craving for recognition as the dominant figure shaping it. When this happens, individuals risk losing their creative potential. Likewise, Nietzsche's concept of the will to power can easily be misinterpreted as a quest for political power, particularly when the focus shifts from self-mastery to the domination of others. Sullivan warned that architects who fail to balance their instincts with their creative energy end up producing frantic, neurotic designs. These architects, he argued, are driven by superficial desires for control and prestige, much like the Nazis with their grandiose plans for Germania.

The idea of the architect as the 'new man' risks becoming more of a symbol of social status or political ideology than an expression of genuine creative talent. Nietzsche cautioned that architects miss the opportunity to excel when 'actors become masters' in society. In such a climate, 'the strength to build' becomes 'paralyzed', leaving great architects increasingly 'disadvantaged' until they are eventually 'made impossible' (GS.356).

There are valuable lessons to learn here for both architects and students beginning to master the trade.

Nietzsche's affirmative philosophy empowers creative individuals, but this power can easily be misused, leading to outcomes that are insipid, toxic, or corrupting. I will conclude this book with seven recommendations, drawn from a Nietzschean perspective, on how to adopt a more meaningful and productive approach to design practice.

Perhaps the most important point to remember is that buildings are not simply structures or containers providing shelter for people and objects. They should go beyond mere functionality, embodying deeper philosophical ideas about life, creativity, and human potential. With this in mind, (1) when designing a building, aim for more than just practicality—create spaces that inspire reflection and personal growth in their users. Additionally, (2) aim to foster creative and cultural renewal in the communities you design for through bold, innovative designs that challenge conventional thinking. This will require you to have confidence in your imaginative abilities to develop a style that is honest to you. If you draw inspiration from historic designs, use them sparingly to avoid diminishing your originality. It is equally important to temper your imagination (as Apollo tempers Dionysus), avoiding overly novel designs that could alienate or confuse others.

Embrace the power of simplicity (3) and use decorative features sparingly. Do not incorporate ornament as appendages but ensure they are integral to the overall unity of the design. Similarly, avoid unnecessary ornament and imposing design features that can distract and draw excessive attention to themselves. A simple and coherent design with a rhythmic play of forms can evoke a powerful presence that puts the user at centre stage but take care not to oversimplify as this can result in predictable, sterile designs that fail to resonate with people. The key lies in finding a balance between order and surprise, or between the Apollonian and Dionysian aspects of design.

Let the natural qualities of construction materials speak for themselves (4). This will help you to create designs that are tactile and textured, and that appeal to a range of senses beyond the visual. It will also foster more instinctive and intimate engagement with the design.

Consider the context of the site and its surroundings to ensure the building complements its environment rather than overshadowing it or blending so much into it that it goes unnoticed (5). Ideally, the building should elevate the broader setting and enhance the architectural character of neighbouring structures.

The architect's ability to focus and discriminate is vital to achieving these goals (6). A productive workspace can aid this, and Nietzsche might suggest taking regular walks or visiting a favourite building or place to reflect on your work. Alternating between different places can offer new perspectives and inform your design ideas. Avoid forcing ideas that are not taking shape by sitting at a desk for extended periods; sometimes stepping away is key to letting creativity flow.

Finally, (7) do not assume that supposed experts or teachers have the answers for your creative designs. Trust your own process. As Zarathustra tells us, 'One repays a teacher badly if one remains only a pupil [...] now I bid you lose me and find yourselves' (Z.I.22[3]: 103).

Recommended reading

Choosing a starting point for reading Nietzsche's works is challenging, largely because his ideas resist systematic organisation, unfolding instead through layers of critique, poetic prose, philosophical 'in jokes', and dense insights that develop across multiple works. Nietzsche's writing can be demanding and challenging, and his critiques of other theories and thinkers may seem harsh or overwhelming to readers who lack familiarity with the philosophical background. Reading his works carefully and reflectively is essential to engage with his ideas effectively. It may help to supplement your reading with introductory guides to Nietzsche's life and ideas, as these provide context for his critiques and can help to clarify difficult passages.

Nietzsche intended *Twilight of the Idols, or, How to Philosophise with a Hammer* (written in 1888, published in 1889) as a good entry point and a summary of his key ideas. It is shorter and more direct than many of his other works, and it offers a relatively accessible overview. Each section reads like an aphorism or short essay, allowing you to dip into his ideas. While densely packed with insights, its brevity provides a useful foundation for more challenging works like *Thus Spoke Zarathustra* (1883–5) and *Beyond Good and Evil* (1886).

For a broader survey of his writings, two excellent compilations of selected excerpts from his major texts are *The Nietzsche Reader*, edited by Keith Ansell-Pearson and Duncan Large (Wiley Blackwell, 2005); and *A Nietzsche Reader: Friedrich Nietzsche*, edited by R.J. Hollingdale (Penguin Classics, 1977).

There are very few works in English that directly explore the relationship between Nietzsche's philosophy and architecture, though there are several important studies in German. They include *Philosophische Flaneur: Nietzsche und die Architektur* (Philosophical Flâneur: Nietzsche and Architecture) by Jörg H. Gleiter (Königshausen & Neumann, 2009); *Nietzsches Italien: Städte, Gärten und Paläste* (Nietzsche's Italy: Cities, Gardens, and Palaces) by Tilmann Buddensieg (Wagenbach, 2002); *Der Klang der Steine: Nietzsches Architekturen* (The Sound of the Stone: Nietzsche's Architectures) by Fritz Neumeyer (Gebr. Mann, 2001); *Der bauende Geist. Friedrich Nietzsche und die Architektur* (The Building Spirit: Friedrich Nietzsche and Architecture) by Markus Breitschmid (Quart-Verlag, 2001); *Ihr Kinderlein kommet: Henry van de Velde, ein vergessenes Projekt für Friedrich Nietzsche* (Your Little Children are Coming: Henry van de Velde, a Forgotten Project for Friedrich Nietzsche) by Thomas Föhl and Alexandre Kostka (Hatje Cantz, 2000); and *Nietzsches Architektur der Erkennenden: Die Welt als Wissenschaft und Fiktion* (Nietzsche's Architecture for the Perceptive: The World as Science and Fiction) by Stephen Griek (Transcript, 2023). In English, two valuable works are *Nietzsche and Architecture: The Grand Style for Modern Living* by Lucy Huskinson (Bloomsbury, 2024), which provides a more comprehensive analysis of Nietzschean ideas in relation to architecture and to several architects discussed in this book; and the anthology *Nietzsche and 'An Architecture of our Minds'*, Alexandre Kostka and Irving Wohlfarth (eds) (Getty Research Institute for the History of Art and the Humanities, 1999). The latter includes essays on various topics under the broad theme of Nietzsche's reception by modernist thinkers, but there are three essays on architecture that I recommend: 'Architecture as Empty Form: Nietzsche and the Art of Building', by Tilmann Buddensieg (1999, pp. 259–84); 'Nietzsche and Modern Architecture', by Fritz Neumeyer (pp. 285–310), which examines the work of Ludwig Mies van der Rohe, Ludwig Hilberseimer, and Bruno Taut; and 'Architecture of the "New Man": Nietzsche, Kessler, Beuys' by Alexandre Kostka (pp. 199–232), which looks briefly at the renovations of Villa Silberblick and the Nietzsche temple-stadium project.

Finally, there are two insightful and engaging works that discuss Nietzsche's life and ideas within the context of the places he lived and visited: *The Good European: Nietzsche's Work Sites in Word and Image* by David Farrell Krell and Donald L. Bates (University of Chicago Press, 2000); and *Friedrich Nietzsche: A Philosophical Biography* by Julian Young (Cambridge University Press, 2010).

References

Ansell-Pearson, K. and Large, D. (eds) (2005) *The Nietzsche Reader*, Wiley Blackwell.

Bachelard, G. (1957/1994) *The Poetics of Space*, Maria Jolas (trans.), Beacon Press.

Baker, E. (1998) 'Richard Wagner and His Search for the Ideal Theatrical Space', in M. Radice (ed.), *Opera in Context*, Amadeus Press, pp. 269–78.

Breitschmid, M. (2001) *Der bauende Geist. Friedrich Nietzsche und die Architektur*, Quart-Verlag.

Buddensieg, T. (1980) 'Das Wohnhaus als Kultban', in P. Schuster, T. Buddensieg and Klaus-Jürgen Sembach (eds), *Peter Behrens und Nürnberg Geschmack Wandel in Deutschland: Historismus, Jugendstil und die Anfänge der Industrieform*, Prestel, pp. 37–47.

Buddensieg, T. (1999) 'Architecture as Empty Form: Nietzsche and the Art of Building', in A. Kostka and I. Wohlfarth (eds), *Nietzsche and 'An Architecture of our Minds'*, Getty Research Institute for the History of Art and the Humanities, pp. 259–84.

Buddensieg, T. (2002) *Nietzsches Italien: Städte, Gärten und Paläste* (Nietzsche's Italy: Cities, Gardens, and Palaces), Wagenbach, 2002.

Burckhardt, J. (1855) *Der Cicerone. Eine Anleitung zum Genuss der Kunstwerke Italiens*, Basel: Schweighauser'sche Verlagsbuchhanglung, 1855. (English: *The Cicerone: An Art Guide to Painting in Italy for the Use of Travellers and Students*, J. Murray, 1879.)

Burckhardt, J. (1867/1987) *The Architecture of the Italian Renaissance*, J. Palmes (trans.), Penguin.

Calderini, C. and Pagnini, L.C. (2015) 'The Debate on the Strengthening of Two Slender Masonry Structures in Early XX Century: A Contribution to the History of Wind Engineering', *Journal of Wind Engineering and Industrial Aerodynamics*, vol. 147: 302–19.

Cimorelli, D. (2016) *Mole Antonelliana Turin: Visitor's Guide*, F. Levi and R. Rolli (eds), Salvana Editoriale.

Cohen, J.-L. (1999) 'Le Corbusier's Nietzschean Metaphors', in A. Kostka and I. Wohlfarth (eds), *Nietzsche and 'An Architecture of Our Minds'*, Getty Research Institute for the History of Art and the Humanities, pp. 311–32.

Cohn, P.V. and Förster-Nietzsche, E. (1931) *Um Nietzsches Untergang: Beiträge zum Verständnis des Genies. Mit einem Anhang von Elisabeth Förster-Nietzsche*, Morris-Verlag.

Easton, L.M. (2006) *The Red Count: The Life and Times of Harry Kessler*, University of California Press.

Föhl, T. and Kostka, A. (2000) *Ihr Kinderlein kommet: Henry van de Velde, ein vergessenes Projekt für Friedrich Nietzsche* (Your Little Children are Coming: Henry van de Velde, a Forgotten Project for Friedrich Nietzsche), Hatje Cantz.

Förster-Nietzsche, E. (1914) *Der einsame Nietzsche*, Alfred Kröner.

Gleiter, J.H. (2009) *Der philosophische Flaneur: Nietzsche und die Architektur*, Königshausen & Neumann.

Griek, S. (2023) *Nietzsches Architektur der Erkennenden: Die Welt als Wissenschaft und Fiktion*, Transcript.

Guillén, M.F. (2006) *The Taylorized Beauty of the Mechanical: Scientific Management and the Rise of Modernist Architecture*, Princeton University Press.

Habel, H. (1970) 'Die Idee eines Festspielhauses', in D. Petzet and M. Petzet (eds), *Die Richard Wagner: Bühne König Ludwigs II*, Prestel, pp. 297–316.

Herrmann, W. (1981) *Gottfried Semper, Theoretischer Nachlass an der ETH Zürich, Katalog und Kommentare*, Birkhäuser.

Hitler, A. (1925/1992) *Mein Kampf*, R. Manheim (trans.), Pimlico.

Hitler, A. (1935/1936) 'Art and Politics', in *Liberty, Art, Nationhood: Three Addresses Delivered at the Seventh National Socialist Congress, Nuremberg*, Müller and Sons, pp. 30–53.

Hollingdale, R.J. (1977) *A Nietzsche Reader: Friedrich Nietzsche*, Penguin Classics.

Huskinson, L. (2024) *Nietzsche and Architecture: The Grand Style for Modern Living*, Bloomsbury.

Jencks, C. (1973) *Le Corbusier and the Tragic View of Architecture*, Penguin Books.

Kessler, H.G. (2011) *Journey to the Abyss: The Diaries of Count Harry Kessler, 1880–1918*. L. Easton (trans.), Knopf.

Kessler, H.G. and van de Velde, H. (2015) *Harry Graf Kessler—Henry van de Velde: Der Briefwechsel*, A. Neumann (ed.), Böhlau.

Kitchen, M. (2017) *Speer: Hitler's Architect*, Yale University Press.

Kostka, A. (1999) 'Architecture of the "New Man": Nietzsche, Kessler, Beuys', in A. Kostka and I. Wohlfarth (eds), *Nietzsche and 'An Architecture of our Minds'*, Getty Research Institute for the History of Art and the Humanities, pp. 199–232.

Kostka, A. and Wohlfarth, I. (eds) (1999) *Nietzsche and 'An Architecture of our Minds'*, Getty Research Institute for the History of Art and the Humanities.

Krell, D.F. and Bates, D.L. (2000) *The Good European: Nietzsche's Work Sites in Word and Image*, University of Chicago Press.

Kühn, P. (1899) 'Studio News. Fritz Schumacher', in *Deutsche Kunst und Dekoration*, vol. 5, pp. 222–7.

Kühn, P. (1904) *Das Nietzsche Archiv zu Weimar*, Alexander Koch.

Lane, B.M. (1985) *Architecture and Politics in Germany: 1918–1945*, Harvard University Press.

Le Corbusier (1923/2016) *Toward an Architecture*, J. Goodman (trans.), Getty Press.

Magirius, H. (1987) *Gottfried Sempers zweites Dresdner Hoftheater*, Büchergilde.

Menocal, N.G. (1981) *Architecture as Nature: The Transcendentalist Idea of Louis Sullivan*, University of Wisconsin Press.

Neumeyer, F. (1999) 'Nietzsche and Modern Architecture', in A. Kostka and I. Wohlfarth (eds), *Nietzsche and 'An Architecture of our Minds'*, Getty Research Institute for the History of Art and the Humanities, pp. 285–310.

Neumeyer, F. (2001/2004) *Der Klang der Stein: Nietzsches Architekturen*, Gebr. Mann Verlag.

Nietzsche, F. (1999) 'Nietzsche and Modern Architecture', in A. Kostka and I. Wohlfarth (eds), *Nietzsche and 'An Architecture of our Minds'*, Getty Research Institute for the History of Art and the Humanities, pp. 285–310.

Nietzsche, F. (1870/2013) *The Greek Music Drama*, P. Bishop (trans.), Contra Mundum Press.

Nietzsche, F. (1872/1993) *The Birth of Tragedy*, S. Whiteside (trans.), Penguin.

Nietzsche, F. (1873–76/2001) *Unfashionable Observations [Untimely Meditations]*, The Complete Works of Friedrich Nietzsche, vol. 2, R.T. Gray (trans.), Stanford University Press.

Nietzsche, F. (1878/1995) *Human, All Too Human I*, The Complete Works of Friedrich Nietzsche, vol. 3, G. Handwerk (trans.), Stanford University Press.

Nietzsche, F. (1880/2013) *The Wanderer and His Shadow*, The Complete Works of Friedrich Nietzsche, vol. 4, G. Handwerk (trans.), Stanford University Press.

Nietzsche, F. (1881/2011) *Dawn [Daybreak]*, The Complete Works of Friedrich Nietzsche, vol. 5, B. Smith (trans.), Stanford University Press.

Nietzsche, F. (1882/2001) *The Gay Science*, J. Nauckhoff (trans.), Cambridge University Press.

Nietzsche, F. (1883–5/1969) *Thus Spoke Zarathustra*, R.J. Hollingdale (trans.), Penguin Books.

Nietzsche, F. (1886/2014) *Beyond Good and Evil/On the Genealogy of Morality*, The Complete Works of Friedrich Nietzsche, vol. 8, A. Del Caro (trans.), Stanford University Press.

Nietzsche, F. (1888/2021) *The Case of Wagner*, in *The Case of Wagner, Twilight of the Idols, The Antichrist, Ecce Homo, Dionysus Dithyrambs, Nietzsche contra Wagner*, The Complete Works of Friedrich Nietzsche, vol. 9, C. Diethe and D. Large (trans.) Stanford University Press, pp. 1–39.

Nietzsche, F. (1908/2021) *Ecce Homo*, in *The Case of Wagner, Twilight of the Idols, The Antichrist, Ecce Homo, Dionysus Dithyrambs, Nietzsche contra Wagner*, The Complete Works of Friedrich Nietzsche, vol. 9, C. Diethe and D. Large (trans.) Stanford University Press, pp. 212–318.

Nietzsche, F. (1994) *Aus meinem Leben*, in Frühe Schriften, vol. 1: Jugendschriften (1854–69), Deutscher Taschenbuch Verlag.

Nietzsche, F. (2003) *Sämtliche Briefe: Kritische Studienausgabe*, 8 vols, Deutscher Taschenbuch Verlag.

Nietzsche, F. (2005) *Sämtliche Werke: Kritische Studienausgabe*, Deutscher Taschenbuch Verlag.

Oehler, R. (1935/1938) *Friedrich Nietzsche und die deutsche Zukunft*, Armanen-Verlag.

Pallasmaa, J. (1996/2005) *The Eyes of the Skin: Architecture and the Senses*, Wiley.

Rohde, E. (1872) *Afterphilologie*, Fritzsch.

Rosenberg, A. (1930/2021) *Nazi Ideology: The Myth of the Twentieth Century*, Blackwells.

Schlemmer, O. (1990) *The Letters and Diaries of Oskar Schlemmer*, Northwestern University Press.

Schultze-Naumburg, P. (1928) *Kunst und Rasse*, Lehmann.

Schumacher, F. (1935/1949) *Stufen Des Lebens: Erinnerungen eines Baumeisters*, Deutsche Verlags-Anstalt.

Scully, V. (1959) 'Louis Sullivan's architectural ornament: A brief note concerning humanist design in the age of force', *Perspecta*, vol. 5: 73–80.

Seidl, A. (1901) *Kunst und Kultur: Aus der Zeit—für die Zeit—wider die Zeit*, Schuster & Loeffler.

Semper, G. (1834/2010) 'Preface to Preliminary Remarks on Polychrome Architecture', in F. Pellizzi (ed.), *The Four Elements of Architecture and Other Writings*, H.F. Mallgrave and W. Herrmann (trans.), Cambridge University Press, pp. 45–73.

Semper, G. (1852/2010) 'Prospectus Comparative Theory of Building', in F. Pellizzi (ed.), *The Four Elements of Architecture and Other Writings*, H.F. Mallgrave and W. Herrmann (trans.), Cambridge University Press: Cambridge: 168–73.

Semper, G. (1860/2004) *Style in the Technical and Tectonic Arts; or Practical Aesthetics*, H.F. Mallgrave and M. Robinson (trans.), Getty Press: Los Angeles.

Semper, G. (1869/2010) 'On Architectural Styles', in F. Pellizzi (ed.), *The Four Elements of Architecture and Other Writings*, H.F. Mallgrave and W. Herrmann (trans.), Cambridge University Press, pp. 264–306.

Semper, M. (1906) *Das Münchener Festspielhaus*, Von Conrad.

Speer, A. (1970/2009), *Inside the Third Reich*, Richard Winston and Clara Winston (trans.), Macmillan.

Stamm, G. (1973–5) 'Monumental Architecture and Ideology: Henry van de Velde's and Harry Graf Kessler's Project for a Nietzsche Monument at Weimar, 1910–1914', *Gentse Bijdragen*, vol. 23: 303–42.

Stephan, B. (1996) *Sächsische Bildhauerkunst: Johannes Schilling, 1828–1910*, Verlag für Bauwesen.

Strauss, D. (1872/2018) *The Old Faith and the New: A Confession*, Hard Press.

Sullivan, L.H. (1892/2014) 'Ornament in Architecture', in *Kindergarten Chats and Other Writings*, Martino, pp. 187–90.

Sullivan, L.H. (1902/2014) 'Education', in *Kindergarten Chats and Other Writings*, Martino, pp. 224–6.

Sullivan, L.H. (1906/2014) 'What Is Architecture: A Study in the American People of Today', in *Kindergarten Chats and Other Writings*, Martino, pp. 227–41.

Taut, B. (1919) *Alpine Architektur des Architekten*, Folkwang-Verlag.

Trodd, C. (2018) 'Revitalizing Romanticism; or Reflections on the Nietzschean Aesthetic and the Modern Imagination', in P. Meecham and D. Arnold (eds), *A Companion to Modern Art*, Wiley, pp. 17–36.

Wagner, R. (1873) *Das Bühnenfestspielhaus zu Bayreuth: Nebst einem Bericht über die Grundsteinlegung desselben*, Fritsch.

Wendland, D. (2007) 'Systematic underestimation of the thrust of vaults among some builders of the 19th century'. Available at: https://elib.unistuttgart.de/bitstream/11682/71/1/Wendland_2007_Thrust_of_vaults.pdf.

van de Velde, H. (1902) 'Die Linie', *Die Zukunft*, 40(49): 385–8.

van de Velde, H. (1995) *Récit de ma vie.1900–1917: Berlin—Weimar—Paris—Bruxelles*, Flammarion.

van de Velde, H. (2003) 'Manuscript on Ornament', E.G. Haddad and R. Anderson (trans.), *Journal of Design History*, 16(2): 139–66.

Van Zanten, D. (2000) *Sullivan's City: The Meaning of Ornament for Louis Sullivan*, W.W. Norton.

von Moos, S. (1968/2009) *Le Corbusier, Elements of a Synthesis*, 010 Publishers.

Whyte, I.B. (1982) *Bruno Taut and the Architecture of Activism*, Cambridge University Press.

Wölfflin, H. (1886/2017) *Prolegomena to a Psychology of Architecture*, M. Selzer (trans.), Keepahead Press.

Young, J. (2010) *Friedrich Nietzsche: A Philosophical Biography*, Cambridge University Press.

Index

Abbe, Ernst 73, 83, 84, 88; see also van de Velde, works: Abbe Ernst monument
aesthetics 2, 3, 55, 111
ancient Greeks/ancient Greek culture 12, 58, 61, 69, 76
Ansell-Pearson, Keith 117
Antonelli, Alessandro 8, 20–21, 48, 64–69, 71, 112; see also Mole Antonelliana
Apollo, Apollonian 8, 12, 15, 20, 22, 30, 35, 36, 41, 43–44, 48, 54–55, 58, 61, 62, 69, 71, 75–76, 79, 89, 106, 107, 109, 115; see also Dionysus, Dionysian
Arc de Triomphe, Paris 102
Ariadne 75–77
Aschheim, Steven E. 3

Bacchus 75; see also Dionysus
Bachelard, Gaston 9
Baroque architecture 16, 19, 20, 30, 38, 76, 112
Basel, Switzerland 64
Basel University 13, 17
Bates, Donald L. 118
Bauhaus, Bauhaus School 3, 54, 70, 99, 103

Bäumler, Alfred 98–99
beauty, beautiful 10, 19, 22, 27, 28, 49, 50, 56, 72, 82
Behrens, Peter 1, 3, 74, 92–93
Behrens, works: book cover for *Thus Spoke Zarathustra* 93; *Hamburger Vorhalle*, Turin 3, 74, 78, 93–94; 'Zarathustra House,' Darmstadt Artist Colony 3, 74, 93
Berlin, Germany 74, 100
Bo Bardi, Lina 1
body 15, 31, 44, 46–47, 52, 62, 82; see also Nietzsche's body; physiological experience/identification
Bolshevik architecture 4, 99–100
Bonn University 11
Breitschmid, Markus 58, 118
Brückwald, Otto 34, 35
Brunelleschi, Filippo 17
Buddensieg, Tilmann 46, 56, 64, 69, 93, 118
Burckhardt, Jacob 17–18, 21, 47; and the Palazzo Pitti 17–18, 53, 54
Burckhardt, works: *Der Cicerone* 17, 47

Caffee Baratti & Milano, Turin 20
Calderini, Chiara 67
Carrera, Pietro 19

cave 14, 15, 26, 31, 74, 78, 93–94, 114
Christianity; Christian buildings 11,
  55, 56
Christine Marie of France 20
Cimorelli, D. 67, 69
classical architecture 69, 76, 101; see
  also neo-classical architecture
Cohen, Jean-Louis 113
Cologne, Germany 64
colossal architecture 47, 54, 101, 102
colour, polychromy 18, 26, 27, 54, 55,
  58–59, 61, 84, 93, 97
crystal, crystal houses 92–97
cultivated philistine 8, 24–25, 30, 33,
  36–39; see also last man/last men

dance 8, 13, 52–55, 62, 83; see also
  rhythm, rhythmic play/form
Darmstadt Colony, Germany 3, 74, 93
degenerate art/architecture 4, 100
Dessau, Germany 100
Deutscher Werkbund 93, 103
Diller, Elizabeth 1
Dionysus/Dionysian 8, 12, 13, 15, 20,
  22, 25, 35, 36, 41, 43–44, 48, 52,
  54–55, 60–62, 69, 71, 75–79, 106,
  107, 109, 110, 112, 115; see also
  Apollo/Apollonian
Durand, Jean-Nicholas Louis 60

eagle 81, 93
Eisenman, Peter 1
empty form 3, 21, 31, 56–57, 60, 69, 118
epic poetry 43

façades 27, 28, 84, 112
Fancelli, Luca 17, 53
festive architecture/experience 8, 48,
  58–60, 69, 75, 77, 106–108
Festspielhaus, Bayreuth 8, 12–13,
  33–36, 39, 77, 79
Festspielhaus, Munich 34, 35, 77
First World War 3, 14, 95
Florence, Italy 7, 17, 21
Föhl, Thomas
Förster, Bernhard 6
Förster-Nietzsche, Elisabeth 6, 21–22, 53
Franco-Prussian war 27
Fuchs, Carl 18

Galleria Subalpina, Turin 19–20
Galleria Vittorio Emanuele II, Milan 19
garden house/pavilion (David Strauss)
  8, 38
Gast, Peter see under Köselitz, Henrich
Gauzentrum, Weimar 105
Genoa, Italy 56, 57
Genoese palazzi, Italy 7, 16–18, 30,
  45–47, 57, 64
German nationalism 6, 99
Germania (Speer) 4, 74, 102, 114
Gesamtkunstwerk 49, 87, 88
Giesler, Hermann 104, 105
glass 3, 19, 35, 68, 74, 84, 85,
  92–97
Gleiter, Jörg H. 65, 68, 118
God, death of 5, 14
Goebbels, Josef 105
Gothic architecture 29, 112

Graf Kessler, Harry 22, 73, 79, 82–85,
   88–90, 92, 106, 108, 118
grandiosity, grandiose architecture 4, 5,
   34, 35, 74, 102, 114
gravity 44, 63
Griek, Stephen 118
Gropius, Walter 54, 93, 112

Hadid, Zaha 1
Hähnels, Ernst Julius 78
Halle, Germany 64
height instinct 11, 15–16, 20–21, 23,
   62–68, 81, 85, 97; see also verticality
Heraclitus 72
herm 87, 88
hero/architect as hero 6, 14, 42, 71, 81,
   89, 98, 101, 107, 113–114
higher man/men 31, 52, 106
Hilberseimer, Ludwig 118
historicism 2, 8, 15
Hitler, Adolf 74, 98–106
Hollingdale, R.J. 117
horizon 9, 16, 22, 30, 54, 62–64, 81
Huskinson, Lucy 118

imitation 7, 8, 25, 27, 34, 38, 45,
   51, 69,
International style 3, 99
Isle of Ischia 15

Jena, Germany 21, 73, 83
Jencks, Charles 113
Jesus 14
Juvarra, Filippo 20

Kant, Immanuel 42
Klinger, Max 88
Köselitz, Heinrich (Peter Gast) 17–19
Kostka, Alexandre 118
Krell, David Farrell 118
Kühn, Paul 47–50, 52, 58, 79

labyrinth 8, 31–33
Large, Duncan 117
last man/last men 24–25; see also
   cultivated philistine
Le Corbusier 1, 14, 71, 93, 112–113
Leipzig University 11, 12
line force (van de Velde) 8, 83

Maillol, Aristide 89
Marie, Christine of France 20
Marie-Jeanne-Baptiste of
   Savoy-Nemours 20
mask, mask-like 27–28, 39
master morality 5, 42–43
master race 6, 99
mausoleum 31, 90
Menocal, Narciso 113
Merleau-Ponty, Maurice 47
Mies van der Rohe, Ludwig 1, 118
Miller Lane, Barbara 100
modernism 3, 5, 103
Mole Antonelliana, Turin 7, 9, 20–22,
   48, 64–69
monumentalism, monumental
   architecture 5, 54, 74, 89, 90, 103
mountain 7, 9, 14–16, 26, 31, 44, 46,
   94, 95, 102, 114

Mount Vesuvius 15
Muses 75, 76, 78
music 12, 13, 17, 18, 38, 43–44, 61, 76, 78; see also Wagner's music
Mussolini, Benito 104, 110

National Museum, Rome 110
National Socialism 6, 74, 97–99, 101, 102, 108, 109; see also Nazi Party; Third Reich
National Theatre, Weimar 104
Naumburg, Germany 10, 21, 64
Nazi architecture 3, 4, 6, 99–105; Volkshalle/People's Hall 102
Nazi Party 3, 6, 97–99, 114; Third Reich 6; see also National Socialism
necessary design 31, 37, 40–42, 49, 55, 58, 59, 89, 115
neo-classical architecture 15, 68
Neumeyer, Fritz 34, 45, 61, 67, 118
Nietzsche archives 6, 21, 47, 73, 79, 81, 82, 88, 104, 105, 108; see also van de Velde, works: Villa Silberblick
Nietzsche, Friedrich: apartments of 15–16, 19, 20, 63; architectural analogies/metaphors of 7, 8, 25, 31–33, 37–39, 65; and construction of model buildings 10; as a flâneur 15, 117; madness/mental breakdown 1, 4, 21; Nietzsche's body 89–90; physical decline of 4, 9, 13, 21; as a prophet 6; as a walker/wanderer 7, 13–15, 17, 22, 65, 78, 106, 111, 115

Nietzsche Memorial Hall, Weimar 74, 78, 97, 102–110
Nietzsche temples 73–74, 78–92
Nietzsche temple-stadium 73, 82–90, 106, 108, 118
Nietzsche, works: *The Antichrist* 5; *The Birth of Tragedy* 12, 43, 61, 75–78; *Daybreak/The Dawn of Day* 56; *Ecce Homo* 1, 65, 73; *The Gay Science/The Joyful Wisdom* 16, 56, 57; *Genealogy of Morals* 72; 'The Greek Music Drama' 61; *Human, All Too Human* 56; *Thus Spoke Zarathustra* 3, 7, 13–14, 24, 47, 64, 65, 74, 78, 92–95, 113, 117; *Twilight of the Idols* 43, 63, 117; *Untimely Meditations* 30; *The Will to Power* 98
nihilism 5, 6, 95
nobility/noble 4, 14, 16–18, 42, 43, 50–52, 63, 68
Nueva Germania, Paraguay 6

Oehler, Adalbert 108, 109
Oehler, Richard 104, 106, 108, 109
ornament/ornamentation 3, 8, 17, 38, 47–52, 75–78, 101, 115; see also empty form
Overbeck, Franz 13

Paestum, Italy see under Temple of Hera
Pagnini, Luisa 67
Palazzi see under Genoa palazzi
Palazzo Berlendis, Venice 15
Palazzo Madama, Turin 20

Palazzo Pitti, Florence 7, 17–18, 53–54, 63, 65
Pallasmaa, Juhani 47
Panathenaic Stadium, Athens 82
Pantheon, Rome 102
philosophizing with a hammer 5
physiological experience/identification 22, 25, 33, 35, 44–47, 50, 52, 55; see also body
Piazza Carlo Alberto, Turin 19, 20
Piazza Castello, Turin 20
Piazza di San Marco, Venice 72
pilgrimage 79, 82, 97, 109,
power 2, 5, 15–18, 76, 79, 98–102, 105, 109, 111, 113–115; see also will to power
Praxiteles of Athens 110
prophet/architect as prophet 6, 14, 71, 111–113

quadriga 75–76

rationalized construction/mindset 7, 8, 11, 12, 22, 25, 26, 33, 38, 40, 43, 56, 58, 61; see also Apollonian
Renaissance architecture 17, 19, 53, 76
ressentiment 100
revaluation of values 24, 51, 95
rhythm, rhythmic play/form 8, 13, 33, 48–55, 58, 62–63, 65, 76, 77, 88, 115; see also dance
Röcken, Germany 9, 10
Rohde, Erwin 30, 77, 78
Romanesque architecture 10, 90, 100

Rosenberg, Alfred 98
Rothenburg ob der Tauber, Germany 30

San Michele, Venice 16
Sauckel, Fritz 108, 109
Savoia-Acaja/House of Savoy 20
Schilling, Johannes 77, 78
Schlemmer, Oskar 54–55; and Triadic Ballet 54–55
Schultze-Naumburg, Paul 74, 78–79, 103–109
Schumacher, Fritz 73, 79–82, 108
Scott Brown, Denise 1
Scully, Vincent 62–63
sculpture 43, 61, 76–78, 87–89, 108
Second World War 34, 98, 105
Seidl, Arthur 81
self-reflection 5, 8, 15, 18, 29, 31–33, 47, 56, 57, 69, 72, 79, 101, 115, 116
Semper, Gottfried 8, 28, 34, 58–62, 71; influence on Nietzsche 28–29, 48, 59–62, 71, 77–78, 112
Semper, Manfred 34
Semper, works: Festspielhaus, Munich 34, 35, 77; 'On Architectural Styles' 61; 'Preliminary Remarks of Polychrome Architecture and Sculpture in Antiquity' 59, 61; Semperoper, Dresden 71, 75–78; *Style in the Technical and Tectonic Arts* 61, 62; Theatre, Rio de Janeiro 77
slave/enslavement 11, 42, 81; see also master morality
Sorrento, Italy 15

Speer, Albert 4, 99–102, 104, 105
Stamm, Günther 82–83
State College for Architecture and
 Crafts, Weimar 103
Strasbourg, France 64
Strauss, David Friedrich 31, 33, 36–38
St. Wenzel church, Naumburg 11, 21
Sullivan, Louis 1, 8, 14, 43, 47–48,
 50–52, 62–63, 71, 101, 113–114
Sullivan, works: Auditorium Tower,
 Chicago 112–113; Guaranty building,
 Buffalo, New York 62–63; 'Ornament
 and Architecture' 50
Sun 84, 94, 97
Superman see under Übermensch
surface 3, 8, 28, 48–50, 55, 58–60, 62,
 68, 90, 101, 102
sustainable architecture 24, 57

Taut, Bruno 1, 3, 92–97, 101, 118
Taut, Max 94
Taut, works: *Alpine Architektur* 94–95;
 Monument des Neuen Gesetzes 3,
 74, 95–97, 101
temple, as architectural type 10, 38,
 57, 72–74, 76, 78, 83, 89, 94, 104;
 see also Nietzsche temples; Nietzsche
 temple-stadium; Temple of Artemis;
 Temple of Hera
Temple of Artemis, Ephesus, Turkey
 10, 72
Temple of Hera, Paestum, Italy 47, 89
theatre, as architectural type see under
 Semper, works; Wagner, works

Third Reich 4, 6, 74, 100, 105; see also
 National Socialism; Nazi Party
tragedy, ancient Greek 12, 61; as
 highest art form 12; see also
 Nietzsche, works: *The Birth of Tragedy*
Trodd, Colin 81
Troost, Paul Ludwig 100, 104
Turin, Italy 3, 7, 9, 18–19, 21, 48, 56,
 57, 64, 66, 68, 74, 93, 94

Übermensch/superman 4–6, 24, 45, 52,
 71, 93, 97, 111, 113
unified style/taste/will 8, 17, 29–30, 33,
 36, 40, 45, 55, 60, 109, 112
unifying instinct 29–30, 100, 109

van de Velde, Henry 1, 8, 22, 47–50, 52,
 58, 62, 73, 79, 82–92, 97, 101, 106,
 108–109, 118
van de Velde, works: 'Die Linie'/'The
 Line' 48, 52; Ernst Abbe Memorial,
 Jena 83–85; Villa Silberblick
 renovations 22, 52, 73, 84–87, 97;
 see also Nietzsche-Archiv; Nietzsche
 temple; Nietzsche temple-complex
Van Zanten, David 52, 113–114
Venice, Italy 15, 65, 72
verticality 76, 84, 85, 90; see also height
 instinct
Villa Rubinacci, Italy 15, 79
Villa Silberblick, Weimar 21–22, 79, 82,
 83, 93, 97, 98, 104, 106, 108–110;
 see also Nietzsche-Archiv, Weimar;
 van de Velde, works

Vitruvius 46–47
völk/völkisch myth 3, 98–99
Volkshalle/People's Hall see under Nazi architecture
von Moos, Stanislaus 113

Wagner, Cosima 62
Wagner, Richard 8, 12–13, 31, 33–36, 39, 43, 58, 62, 65, 77, 79, 104; Nietzsche's rejection of 8, 12–13, 15, 31, 33–36, 39, 56, 65, 112; Wagner's music 12, 33–35, 112
Wagner, works: *Die Meistersinger* 77; see also Festspielhaus, Bayreuth; Munich Theatre
war see under First World War; Second World War
Weimar, Germany 22, 47, 73, 74, 83, 86, 87, 91, 97, 100, 103–107, 110
Wendlend, David 67

Wilamowitz-Möellendorf, Ulrich von 78
will to power 2, 4, 5, 7, 8, 15, 16, 22, 24, 29, 32, 39–53, 55–56, 60, 62–64, 67, 69, 71, 78, 81, 98–100, 102, 109, 111, 112, 114
will to truth 7, 11, 24–25, 32, 42, 81
Wohlfarth, Irving 118
Wölfflin, Heinrich 46
Woods, Lebbeus 1

Young, Julian 118

Zarathustra 14, 15, 20, 25, 26, 31, 52, 64, 71, 73, 74, 78, 79, 81, 84, 92–93, 97–99, 101, 106, 107, 109, 113–114, 116; Zarathustra's animals/companions see under eagle; see also Peter Behrens, works: 'Zarathustra House'; Nietzsche, works: *Thus Spoke Zarathustra*

For Product Safety Concerns and Information please contact our EU representative GPSR@taylorandfrancis.com
Taylor & Francis Verlag GmbH, Kaufingerstraße 24, 80331 München, Germany

www.ingramcontent.com/pod-product-compliance
Lightning Source LLC
Chambersburg PA
CBHW051542230426
43669CB00015B/2700